TALLYNS
OF
ENGLAND AND AMERICA:
A HISTORY AND GENEALOGY
(1080-1979)

The Descendants of William R. Tallyn
of
Stoke Rivers, Devonshire, England

By
DONN L. COCHRAN

JANAWAY PUBLISHING
2015

Tallyns of England and America: A History and Genealogy (1080-1979).
The Descendants of William R. Tallyn of Stoke Rivers, Devonshire, England

Originally self-published
1980

Reprinted by:

Janaway Publishing, Inc.
732 Kelsey Ct.
Santa Maria, California 93454
(805) 925-1038
www.JanawayGenealogy.com

2015

ISBN: 978-1-59641-348-1

Reprinted with the kind permission of Annetta Cochran, wife of the author, Donn L. Cochran.

Made in the United States of America

TALLYNS OF ENGLAND AND AMERICA

A HISTORY AND GENEALOGY

(1680-1979)

The Descendants of William R. Tallyn

Of

Stoke Rivers Devonshire, England

By

Donn L. Cochran

1980

i

TABLE OF CONTENTS

****

DEDICATION

This work is dedicated to the following most senior Tallyn Descendants *

1. Ethel Leta (Kindig) Liebers
   B. July 25,1888
2. Fern V. (Pickard)Piche'
   B. May 6,1889
3. Vida G. (Davis)Davison
   B. October 31,1891
4. Emory O. Forney
   B. July 11,1893
5. Lelia May (Kindig) Thompson
   B.February 3,1894
6. Leslie Owen Kindig
   B. February 28,1897

7. Ella May (Tallyn) Tibbetts
   B. March 4, 1897
8. Roy Cranston Forney
   B. July 18, 1898
9. Albert William Lee
   B. November 12,1899
10. Ruth (Kindig) Hamilton
    B. November 4 , 1900
11. Franklin McCue Tallyn
    B. September 12, 1902
12. Lloyd Emmett Tallyn
    B. October 12, 1903

****

ACKNOWLEDGEMENTS

The author wishes to acknowledge those individuals whose interests and efforts have greatly contributed to this work. He is most indebted to Emory Owen Forney of Minonk, Illinois. Mr Forney provided a major portion of the historical, genealogical and biographical data for many descendants but particulary the descendants of Anthony and Susanna (Lee) Tallyn.

Special acknowledgement is due Mrs. Ella (Tallyn) Tibbetts of Edwards, Illinois who served as a principal biographer and consultant for the family and descendants of Thomas R. and Elizabeth (Fry) Tallyn.

Major contributors to the segment on the family and descendants of Joseph and Sarah (Daniel) Tallyn include:

Edwin W. Tallyn of Walnut Creek, California: who contributed data for the family and descendants of William H. and Mabel(Ellison) Tallyn.
Verna (Tallyn)Herbst of Washington, Illinois: for her assistance with the descendants of Arthur H. and Anna(Heiken) Tallyn.
Mrs. Gracele(Kindig)McPherson of Lincoln,Nebraska: who was most helpful concerning the descendants of Charles S. and Lizzie (Tallyn) Kindig.
Sheldena (Lee) Litle of Harrisonville,Missouri: a major contributor for the family of Herschel and Sarah (Tallyn) Lee.
Mrs. Donald Wolf(Arlene Tallyn) of Benson, Illinois: the major biographer for the family of Newton and Mary (Eckhart) Tallyn.
Mrs. Harry G. Thompson (Lelia May Kindig) of Bakersfield, California: for her help with the descendants of Theodore H. and Alice (Tallyn) Kindig.

Milford G. Tallyn of St. Louis, Missouri: provided much of the historical, biographical and genealogical data for the family and descendants of Frederick Newton and Emilie (Fry) Tallyn.

Mrs. Lawrence Liebers of Lincoln, Nebraska: for her assistance with the family of Otto H. and Ethel Leta (Kindig) Liebers.

---

* Listing is based on data received by the author as of December 1979.

INTRODUCTION

Part I: The initial section is concerned with the origins of the Tallyn
surname. It spans the period between The Norman Conquest (1080) and the
mid-1500's. The latter date marks the period when individuals assumed
or were given surnames to facilitate the needs of political and ecclesiastical institutions..The former date marks the period when the Normans
of Normandy (France) settled areas of present day Cornwall and Devon
Counties of England. Records (15th century) indicate descendants of these
Norman conquerors who settled this area, began to use the place name of
" Talland " (i.e., the village of Talland, Cornwall) as their surname.

Part II: This section attempts to forge a genealogical link between William
R. Tallyn of Stoke Rivers and early Tallyns of 1700 North Devon. Birth,
Christening and Marriage records provide the major data source for this
effort. The general fragmentation of data for this period, however,
has served to complicate this task and present threats to validity.

Part III: The central focus here is the children and descendants of
William R. Tallyn of Stoke Rivers. The first section deals with those
who remained in England and the second, their "American Cousins" who
settled in America. It is difficult to envision the conditions and
events which caused the latter descendants to leave their scenic Devon
and join the great wave of immigrants to America.
     By 1800 the best farm land had long been acquired and put under culti-
vation. The eldest son of the family could expect to work the land and
some day own it. For others,less favored by circumstances of birth,the
future, at best,was bleak. In America there was the promise of a new
beginning and prosperity associated with the ownership of land.
     There is good evidence the first Tallyns to settle in America follow-
ed the classic "brother pattern" of immigration. The brothers, usually
three or four elect the oldest amongst them to visit the country of
interest for the purpose of assessing its potential for meeting the
needs of each. In most instances he went to a specific geographical
area where friends and relatives have previously settled. The search for
fertile and inexpensive land usually ended at the edge of the rapidly
expanding frontier. The news of a positive assessment prompted the remaining brothers to begin preparations for the voyage to America.

Part IV: It is difficult to present a meaningful and full account of
Tallyn descendants without reference to the families of individuals
allied with the Tallyn Line my marriage. This section (Appendices)
contains brief "thumb-nail sketches" of historical and genealogical
interest for several such families. The reader is urged to consult
the appropriate appendix where there is an indepth interest in a
specific allied family.

     In conclusion, it is noted that the various sections of this
work are inter-related. Initial sections provide a framework for de-
riving a greater understanding and appreciation of data contained in
later sections.
                         ****

I.

THE TALLYN SURNAME

Some Historical Considerations

Tallyn is but one of many variant spellings of Talland which first appears as a place name in Domesday Book (Vol I) of 1085 Cornwall. Talland is the name of a small village near the coast of Cornwall. Talland and its many alternative spellings, including Tallyn, is of Celtic origin. The Celtic language is the origin of the language of modern Wales, Cornwall and Brittany. It is of interest to note that, in the eighth century, the area comprising the present day counties of Cornwall and Devon, England was known as West Wales. This, in part, accounts for the many family and place names of Celtic origin found there and listed in the Domesday Book of William The Conqueror.

Another spelling of the Tallyn surname is found as a place name in S.W. Merioneth County, Wales. In Merioneth is the town of Talyllyn. It lies at the head of Talyllyn Lake in beautiful Talyllyn Valley. The suffix lyn and later linn refers to lake, pond or a body of water. In Merioneth, Talyllyn literally means,"the town at the head of the head of the lake. The suffix lyn is also present in the North Devon rivers of East and West Lyn. The linn variation appears in the port city of Tallinn of Estonia (USSR).

Family surnames grew out of the need to facilitate the conduct of political and ecclesiastical record keeping. Surnames were often derived from some outstanding physical trait or characteristic, occupation or place of birth or residence. Records of 15th century Cornwall show that individuals residing at Talland and nearby Morthe have assumed these place names as surnames, for example, John of Talland and Hugh of Morthe, became known as John Talland and Hugh Morthe.

Time and usage has brought about many alternative spellings of the Talland surname. Some of the most common spellings on Cornwall Parish records between 1450 and 1870 include: Tallyn, Talling, Tallin, Tallen, Tallent, Tallon, Tallonde, Tallond, Talloon, Tallande, Tallett, Tallatt, Tallente and Tallante.

In North Devon, England, during this same time interval, Tallin, Tallen, Talling and Taling seems to have been the preferred spellings. The spelling Tallyn appears on the parish records of North Devon in 1629. By the 1800's it is the most favored spelling of those families residing in the Barnstaple area.

Some Tallands of Early Cornwall: Talland is part of the Parish of Talland. It is located on the Bay of Talland about eight miles south of Liskear. The Parish was established in 1190 under the Diocese of Exeter (Devon) and Archdeaconry of Cornwall. The Parish appears to be named after a rather obscure 3rd century saint, St. Tallanus, who was instrumental in making Cornwall free of demons and snakes. The Domesday Book lists the town as Portatlant. Portatlant (Talland), as a place name, constitutes the earliest record of the family surname, known to the author. It appears in, Domesday Book Vol I (1085), as an entry under the holdings of Robert, the Count of Mortain as follows:

"...The Count has 1 manor which is called Portatlant(Talland) which Leueron held T.R.E. and it rendered geld for 1 ferling.

3

A HISTORY OF
THE COUNTY OF
CORNWALL

EDITED BY

WILLIAM PAGE F.S.A.

Part 8

THE DOMESDAY SURVEY FOR CORNWALL

THE HOLDERS OF LANDS

60 acres of wood(land) and 300 acres of pasture. And it is worth 15 *li.* and 1 mark of silver and 5*s.* yearly, and when the Count received it it was worth 30*li.*

The Count has 1 manor which is called TRIB[ER]TAN, *Exch.* TRIBERTHA [Trebartha in North Hill], which Ulnod held T.R.E., wherein is half a hide, and it rendered geld for 1 ferling. Four teams can plough this. Turstin holds this of the Count. There Turstin has in demesne half a ferling and half a plough and the villeins (have) the remaining land and 3 ploughs. There Turstin has 2 villeins and 6 bordars. And it is worth 15*s.* yearly, and when the Count received it it was worth the same amount.

The Count has 1 manor which is called HIRMENEU, *Exch.* ERMENHEU [? Harmony in Tamerton] which Levenot held T.R.E., wherein is 1 virgate, and it rendered geld for half a virgate. Six teams can plough this. Levenod holds this of the Count. There Levenod has in demesne half a virgate and half a plough, and the villeins (have) the remaining land. There Levenod has 5 bordars and 2 serfs and 15 acres of wood(land) and 20 acres of pasture. And it is worth 5*s.* yearly, and when the Count received it it was worth 15*s.*

held T.R.E. and it rendered geld for half a ferling. One team can plough this. Hamelin holds this of the Count and he has there 1 villein and 1 bordar and 40 acres of pasture. And it is worth 3*s.*, and when (the Count) received it (it was worth) 5*s.*

*The Count has 1 manor which is called PORTATLANT [Talland] which Leueron held T.R.E. and it rendered geld for 1 ferling. Two teams can plough this. Odo holds this of the Count and he has there 2 bordars and 1 serf

fol. 265.

and 4 acres of pasture. And it is worth 2*s.*, and when (the Count) received it (it was worth) 7*s.*

fol. 334*b.*

LAND OF JUHELL IN CORNWALL

Juhell [*Exch.* Judhel de Totenais] has 1 manor which is called FORCHETESTAN [Forkstone in Whitstone] which Alward held T.R.E. And now Turstin the Sheriff holds it of Juhell. Therein are 3 ferlings and it rendered geld for

Two teams can plough this. Odo holds this of the Count and
he has there 2 bordars and 4 acres of pasture. And it is
worth 2s(shillings),and when(the Count)received it(it was
worth) 7s."

Unfortunately, <u>Domesday Book</u> rarely enters into details of manorial
history. Leueron may have been a soldier under William The Conqueror who
was awarded the manor for service to The Conqueror. The typical manor of
this period was held by a lord who came by it through inheritance or
service to The Conqueror.

Little is known of the " Lords of Talland Manor" for the years spanning
the interval between 1085 and the mid 1400's. Genealogical records of the
Morthe (Murth) family of Talland indicate that, Joano, the daughter of
John and Johan(Penquite) Talland, married John Murth, the son of Hugh and
Constance(Knight) Murth of Talland. Joano (Talland) Murth was heir to the
Talland Manor and lands and with her the estate passed to the Murth line.
Murth descendants resided at Talland Manor until the death of Jeffery
Morthe (Murth), the last male of the line.

Margery, the daughter and heiress of Jeffery Morthe, married John
Woollcombe of Ashbury (Devon,England). John is the Sheriff of Ashbury.
There is no reference made to Talland Manor in the Woollcombe genealogy.
The heraldy of the Morthe-Woollcombe lines is contained in the Woolla-
combe coat-of-arms. The Talland coat-of arms is registered with the
College-of-Arms (England).

The first record, found by the author, of Talland spelled as <u>Tallyn</u>
appears in the parish christening records of Bodmin a village not far
from Talland, Cornwall. The entry reads as follows:

       "....Jays Tallyn christened, August 3, 1587, the son
       of Richard Tallyn."

Tallands of 16th century Cornwall resided in about seven small
villages located some twenty miles of each other. A parish entry
for one of those villages, St. Winnow,reads as follows:

       ".....Constance Tallyn christened, February 26,1637,
       the daughter of John and Temperance Tallyn."

<u>Some Tallands of Early Devon</u>: During the time of William The
Conqueror much of Devon (Devrescira) has held under The Sheriff of
Baldwin and Count Robert of Mortain. An entry in <u>Domesday Book, Vol I</u>
shows Count Robert holding a manor called Bratona which included the
present day villages of Bratton Fleming and Stoke Rivers.

Since the mid 1500's individuals of the Talland (Tallyn) surname
have tended to cluster in a number of villages within a ten mile
radius of Barnstaple of North Devon.   A large group of individuals
made their homes in the villages of Parracombe, Shirwell, Loxhore,
Challacombe, Bratton Fleming, Stoke Rivers and Brayford just East and
Northeast of Barnstaple. An early entry in the marriage records of
nearby Berrynabor reads:

       ".....William Tallin married Eleanor Nichols in 1579."

In Barnstaple and villages to the Southwest, the favored spelling
of the family surname is <u>Tallin</u>. In villages to the Southeast of
Barnstaple <u>Tallyn</u>, <u>Tallin</u> and <u>Tallen</u> are most preferred by individuals of this area.   By 1800 <u>Tallyn</u> is preferred by those
residing in villages North and Northeast of Barnstaple.

<u>John</u> is the most common name found for male Tallyn descendants follow-
ed by <u>William</u>,<u>Thomas</u>,<u>Phillip</u> and <u>Robert</u>. <u>Elizabeth</u> and <u>Mary</u> were the
most favored for females followed by <u>Ann</u>, <u>Sarah</u>,<u>Susanne</u> and <u>Susanna(h)</u>.

****

VISITATIONS OF CORNWALL,

COMPRISING

THE HERALDS' VISITATIONS OF 1530, 1573, & 1620.

MORTHE OF TALLAND. p. 331

ARMS :—Arg. a lion rampant between three fleurs-de-lis, Gu.

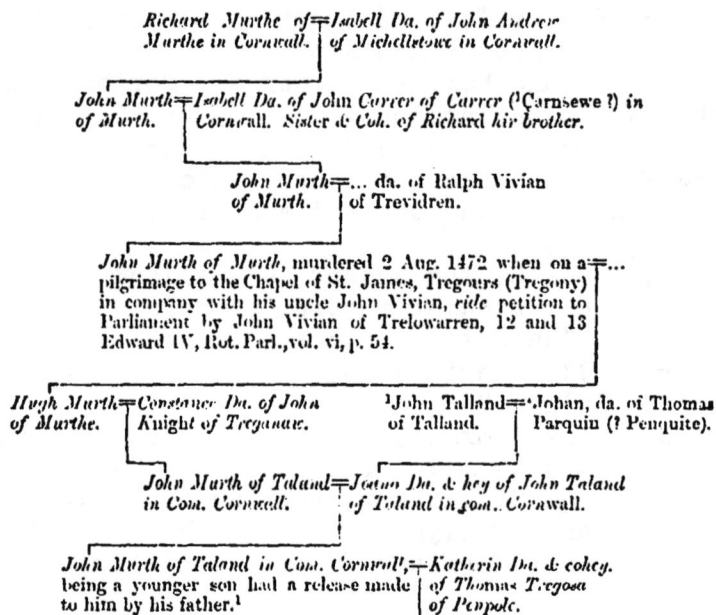

Richard Murthe of=Isabell Da. of John Andrew
Murthe in Cornwall. | of Michelletowe in Cornwall.

John Murth=Isabell Da. of John Carrer of Carrer (?Carnsewe ?) in
of Murth. | Cornwall. Sister & Coh. of Richard hir brother.

John Murth=... da. of Ralph Vivian
of Murth. | of Trevidren.

John Murth of Murth, murdered 2 Aug. 1472 when on a=...
pilgrimage to the Chapel of St. James, Tregours (Tregony)
in company with his uncle John Vivian, vide petition to
Parliament by John Vivian of Trelowarren, 12 and 13
Edward IV, Rot. Parl.,vol. vi, p. 54.

Hugh Murth=Constance Da. of John   ¹John Talland=Johan, da. of Thomas
of Murthe. | Knight of Treganan.   of Talland. | Parquin (? Penquite).

John Murth of Taland=Jeane Da. & hey of John Taland
in Com. Cornwall. | of Taland in com.. Cornwall.

John Murth of Taland in Com. Cornwall,=Katherin Da. & cohey.
being a younger son had a release made | of Thomas Tregosa
to him by his father.¹ | of Penpole.

pp. 206—207

MURTH of Talland, and St. Stephen's.—This family, whose original name was Randall, is said to have been seated at Bodenna, in the time of Richard II. The little however, that may be traced with respect to a private family, in those early times, must be generally considered as resting on unsettled foundations. In the time of Carew, the Murths were resident in the manor house of Talland, which came to the family by an heiress of that name, and held considerable estates in the parish of Trenegloss, and also in St. Stephen's, near Launceston; which property, it is supposed, came to one of the family by his marriage with Elizabeth, daughter and coheiress of Nicholas Jeffery, of Launceston, who was buried in the family vault at Talland, in 1687.

Jeffery Murth, the last of the male line, left issue a daughter and heiress, who was married in 1748, to John Woollcombe, of Ashbury, in Devon, esq.

Arms.—Argent, a lion rampant, between three fleur-de-lis, gules. See arms of Woollcombe, plate XXIII.

PART II

William R. Tallyn and Some Early Tallyns of Stoke Rivers and Bratton Felming:

The focus of this section is to forge a generational link between early Tallyns of Stoke Rivers and Bratton Fleming and Tallyns of this same area thought to be the ancestors of William R. Tallyn of Birch Farm of Stoke Rivers.

The scarcity of records for this period (1600-1750) makes generational linkage hazardous, at best. The major source of data underlying this effort stems from municipal and parish records of births, christenings, marriages and deaths. Time, weather and war have destroyed many of these valuable records. The information and data presented below must be considered in light of these hazards and limitations.

A brief glance at a detailed map of Barnstaple and the surrounding areas of Stoke Rivers, Bratton Fleming, Birch, Davis, Loxhore &Challacombe shows them within a few miles of each other. All represent communities long associated with Tallyn descendants of North Devon. The development and usage of family surnames, as indicated in the previous section, complicates the already complex task of genealogy research in this area. The Tallyn spelling has generally held for the families of this limited area. However, instances do exist where children of the same family are listed under Tallyn , Tallen or Tallin.

William R. Tallyn: Some Genealogical Considerations:

Marriage records for Bratton Fleming show the following entry:

(I)   Richard Tallyn married Mary Cormer (1629)

This entry is of interest in that it constitutes one of the earliest records for a Tallyn in this area. Subsequent records show additional ties between the two families.

Richard has been assigned the number one (1) position in this tentative ancestory of William R. Tallyn. The marriage date of Richard and Joan indicate they were likely born around 1605 and 1607, respectively.

(II) Thomas Tallyn: Thomas appears to be a descendant of Richard and Mary (Cormer)Tallyn Thomas married Joan Cormer. The marriage (April 18, 1657) is recorded under Thomas Tallin and Tallyn. The 1657 marriage indicates Thomas and Joan were born around 1635 and 1637, respectively. The general absence of data for this period makes it difficult to verify the relationship (if any) between Richard (I) and Thomas (II). The circumstantial evidence underlying a possible connection stems from the spelling of the surname, birth and place of marriage (Barnstaple area) data. It also seems unusual that both married spouses of the same family surname of Cormer.

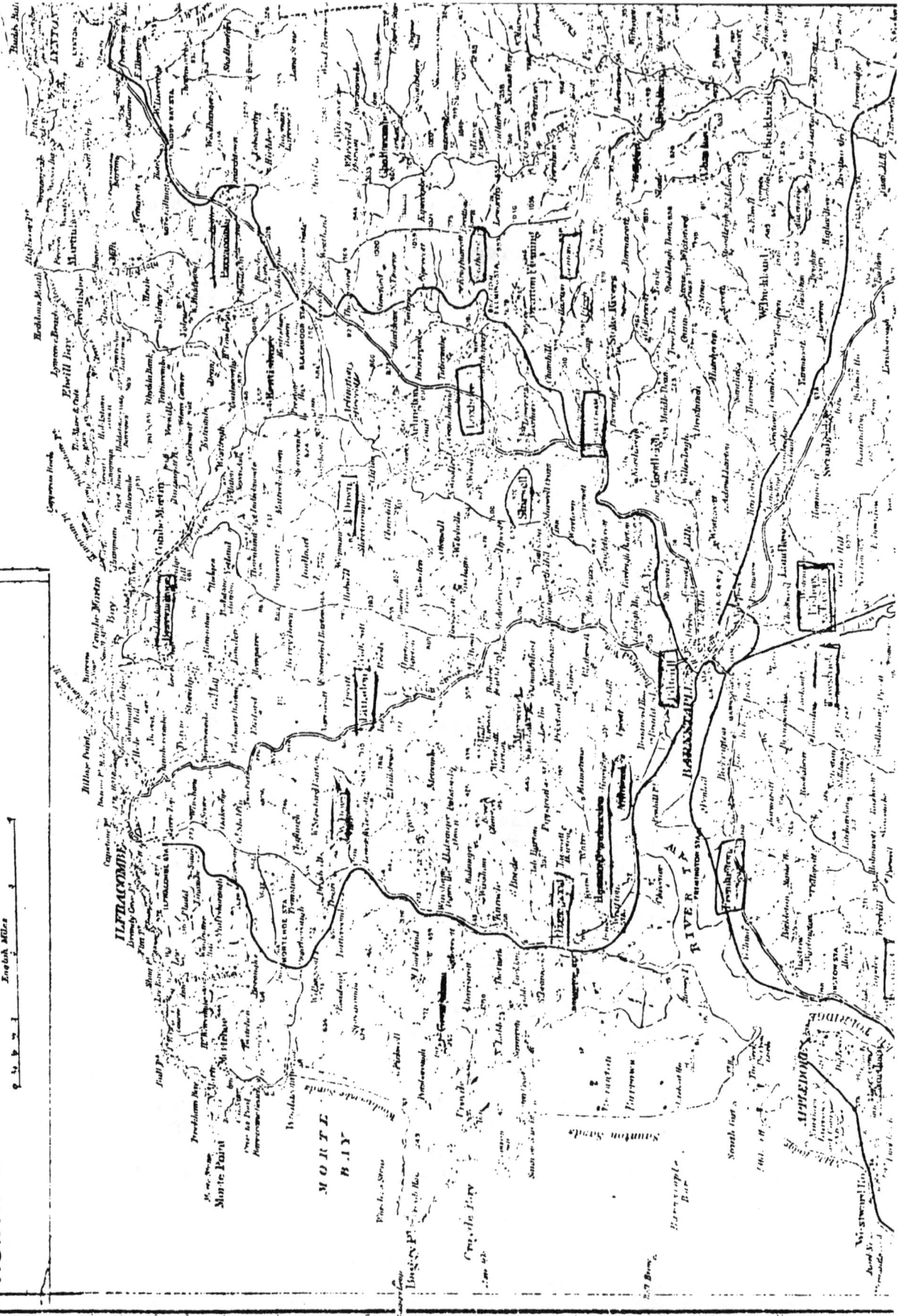

English Miles

(III) Richard Tallyn: According to the available data, Richard appears to be the best candidate at the third generation level. Evidence supporting this choice is circumstantial. Richard is from Stoke Rivers. About 1705 he married a woman named Petronell. Stoke Rivers parish records indicate they had at least six children. They are listed along with the year of christening: Sarah (1709), Edith (1712), Susannah(1715), Richard (1717) and Thomas (1718). This data suggests that Richard and Petronell were married around 1708. This would indicate they were born around 1675 and 1677, respectively.

(IV) Thomas Tallyn: Evidence favors Thomas (1718) over Richard(1717) at the fourth generation level. Various records for Stoke Rivers and the surrounding area fail to show any further entries for Richard indicating he may have died prior to reaching adulthood or took up residence in a county other than Devon.

Thomas (1718) remained in Devon where he married a woman by the name of Mary. Thomas and Mary made their home at Bratton Fleming. Parish records show at least two children, John (1758) and Thomas (1759), were born to the marriage. This christening data is a bit confusing. It would appear that Thomas and Mary were either married in their late 30's or that christening records for the family are incomplete.

****

Data at this point with respect to the lineage of William R. Tallyn improves substantially, becoming less circumstantial and more evidential in nature.

(V) Thomas Tallyn: Thomas (1759) and his brother, John (1758), were both born in Bratton Fleming where they grew to manhood, married and raised their respective families.

John married a woman named, Thomasin. Their children included: John (1779), Thomas(1782), Mary(1787), and Betsy Tallyn (1796). Betsy married (June 18,1817) Henry Isaac. John Tallyn (1799) was a school master of the Pauper School of Bratton Fleming.

Marriage records show Thomas Tallyn married(March26,1787) Charity Pugsley. They were married at nearby Loxhore. Charity was the daughter of Anthony and Mary Pugsley of Loxhore. Parish record for Loxhore shows that Charity was christened, March 29,1767. Thomas and Charity made their home at Bratton Fleming. Christening records for the parish indicate at least five children were born to the marriage. They are listed along with their date of christening:

(a) William Tallyn: Jan. 5, 1788
(b) Mary Tallyn: Feb. 28, 1791
(c) Elizabeth Tallyn:Mar. 13,1793
(d) Ann Tallyn: Sept. 16, 1795
(e) John Tallyn: July 15, 1798

The 1841 census for Stoke Rivers lists Charity Tallyn, age 74 (widow) under the household of William Tallyn (1788). This indicates Thomas (1759) died prior to the taking of this census. Charity does not appear on the 1851 or subsequent census. This suggests she died prior to 1851.

There is an entry in the <u>Barnstaple Register of Deaths,</u> which may refer to William's brother, John Tallyn (1798).

(deceased) <u>John Tallyn</u> age 74 1st quarter(Jan.-March) of 1874.

****

IV. <u>William R. Tallyn:</u> In light of this proposed lineage, it is probable that the middle initial <u>R</u> in William's name stands for <u>Richard</u>. The earliest record for William is the Bratton Fleming christening record of 1788. This same source indicates William married a woman named, Mary. William and Mary first made their home in Bratton Fleming where two of their children were born.

<u>William Tallyn:</u> (C) April 15, 1815
<u>James Tallyn:</u> (C) November 10, 1816

It is important to note that up to this point in time the family were members of the <u>Church of England.</u> The christening records listed in this document stem from this source. Shortly after the birth of James Tallyn (1816) the family removed to Burch (Birch) of the Parish of Stoke Rivers. Parish records for the Church of England at Stoke Rivers do not list the eight additional children born to William and Mary. There is good evidence that the family may have joined the Baptist Church of Stoke Rivers. This would account for the absence of christening records for the remaining children of William and Mary Tallyn. They include: <u>John</u> (1818), <u>Thomas</u> (1820),<u>Ann</u> (1821), <u>George</u> (?), <u>Anthony</u> (1823), <u>Mary</u> (1826), <u>Joseph</u> (1829) and <u>Elizabeth</u> (1832).

Mary, the wife of William is not enumerated on the 1841 census for Stoke Rivers along with other members of the family. This census lists the family as follows:

<u>William Tallyn</u>	age 53	Farmer	B. Devonshire
Charity	74	(widow)	"
William	26		"
James	24		"
John	23		"
Thomas	21		"
Ann	20		"
Mary	15		"
Elizabeth	9		"

****

The absence of Mary, the wife of William, from the 1841 (and subsequent) census presents a dilemma. Normally, the absence of an individual for the census indicates the person died prior to the taking of the census. Historically, men have picked spouses one or two years their junior. If so, Mary would have been born around 1790. Accordingly, she would have been about age 51 in 1841. The death notice of Joseph Tallyn indicates his father died at age 75 and his mother age 74.

The 1851 census for Bratton Fleming lists William (a widower) age 63 residing in the town of Bratton of Bratton Fleming. Wm R. Tallyn does not appear on subsequent North Devon census years.

The scarcity of records makes it difficult to resolve this data inconsistency. The Barnstaple Register of Deaths, contains the following entries of interest:

Mary Tallyn: (died) 1837 3rd Quarter (July-Sept.)

William Tallyn: "   1859 1st Quarter (Jan.-March)

****

The children and descendants of William R. and Mary Tallyn are presented on the following pages. The central concern is the listing of those children who settled in America and their descendants. In the process of researching these descendants a limited amount of data was accumulated for those descendants who remained in England.This data, while fragmented and incomplete is presented in Section A of Part III.

Section B of Part III contains data for children and descendants who settled in America. It is important to note Mary (Tallyn)Ridd did not herself settle in America but her husband and some of her children did. Data for her children and descendants is presented with the group who settled in America.

****

Of Genealogical Interest

The table below shows the number of descendants of 3 children of William R..Tallyn of Stoke Rivers. The entries are based on data available to the author as of December 3, 1979. Data for Thomas R. Tallyn is incomplete.

	Children	Grand Children	Gt. Gr Children	$Gt^2Gr.$ Children	$Gt3Gr.$ Children	TOTALS
Thomas R. Tallyn	8	23	22	15	_____	68
Anthony Tallyn	7	22	57	64	33	183
Joseph Tallyn	10	38	66	109	34	257
TOTALS	25	83	145	188	67	508

(Those Descendants Who Remained in England)

CHILDREN AND DESCENDANTS OF WILLIAM R. AND MARY TALLYN
OF
STOKE RIVERS
DEVON,ENGLAND

****

I. WILLIAM TALLYN: [1]

William was the first child born to William and Mary Tallyn.
Christening records of Bratton Fleming indicate William was christened, May 21, 1815. Shortly after , around 1818, the family moved
to Birch Farm of the Parish of Stoke Rivers.
About 1844 he married a woman named Mary. Mary was born around
1816 (Devon). William and Mary made their home at Rye Park of
Bratton Fleming, where they owned and operated a farm of 113 acres.
Seven children were known to have been born to the marriage. They
are listed below along with their year of birth estimated from
census data. They were all born in Bratton Fleming and include:

   William Tallyn (1845), Thomas (1846), James (1848), Anthony
   (1850), Alice (1851), Joseph (1854) and Selina Tallyn (1859).
The 1871 census for Bratton Fleming shows the following children
still living at home with William (age 54) and Mary (age 54).

   William (26),Thomas (24), James(22), Anthony(21), Alice(20)
   & Selina(12).
The boys are shown helping with the farm. Selina is attending
school and Alice helping at home.
   Little additional information exists for the family. Three
members of the family are known to be buried at Stoke Rivers.
The tradition of up-rooting headstones older than one hundred
years complicates the task of identifying individuals who
pre-date this time interval. It is quite likely , William R. and
Mary Tallyn are buried at Stoke Rivers in addition to the following:

   William Tallyn (1845) , died,Feb.18,1923 (age 77).

   James Tallyn: (1848), died Dec.8, 1925(age 77).

   Selina Tallyn: (1859), died Nov.12,1918 (about age 60).

   The obituary of John Tallyn, the brother of William (1815) of
this section, indicates William died prior to 1902 (John's year
of death). One source indicates William died, February 11, 1888.
The Barnstaple Registry of Deaths contains the following entry:

   (deceased) William Tallyn: age 72 1st.Quarter (Jan.Feb.)1888.

****

[1] Sources for this section include the 1841,1851,1861 and 1871
   census for Bratton Fleming and Stoke Rivers. The author is also
   indebted to W. Edwin Tallyn of Walnut Creek, California, for
   making his notes on(Stoke Rivers) burials available.

II. JOHN TALLYN: [1]

John, the son of William R. and Mary Tallyn, was born, May 14, 1818. He was born and raised at Birch Farm of the Parish of Stoke Rivers. In 1843 John married Mary A. Brownscombe. Their marriage is recorded in, Barnstaple Book of Marriages, Vol. X p. 42, 1843.

Mary was the eldest daughter of five daughters and five sons born to Thomas and Mary Ann Brownscombe of South Haxton Barton (town) of Bratton Fleming. Mary's siblings are listed along with their year of christening.(Bratton Fleming Christening Records)

Mary Ann(Brownscombe) Tallyn was christened, Feb.11,1823. Her siblings include: Thomas(1819),William(1821),John(1824),Ann (1826), Kitty(1828),Sarah(1830),James(1833),Edward(1835 and Grace Brownscombe(1837).

John and Mary Tallyn set up residence on a farm at West Haxton of Bratton Fleming. Mary Ann (1844), John (1846), James (1848) and Thomas Tallyn(1851)were born at West Haxton.

The 1861 census for Bratton Fleming shows the family on a 26 acre farm at Lower Haxton. Six additional children are listed on this census including: William(1853), Elizabeth(1854),Susanna (1856), Hannah(1858), Anthony(1860) and Joshua (after 1861). Another child(daughter) was born after 1861. She died about 1872 (age ?) and was buried at the Baptist Chapel cemetery at Brayford.

The family lived for a time at Lower Cowley in the nearby Parish of Kentisbury, prior to settling (about 1868) in the town of (barton) Charles. John Tallyn was a Baptist and a preacher of considerable ability. He often preached at the Baptist Chapel at Braford.

Mary (Brownscombe) Tallyn died, June 15,1884 (age 63), at Charles. John Tallyn died, May 14, 1902 at Charles, after a brief illness. Both are buried in the Baptist Chapel cemetery at nearby Brayford.

John was survived by ten of his children. His obituary notice lists them as follows:

> John of Bolton,James of Derby Abbey,Thomas of Bristol, William of Wakefield,Anthony, Joshua and Mary Ann of Charles, Elizabeth (Mrs. Skinner) of Stoke Rivers,Susanna (Mrs. Tallyn) of Rye Park and Hannah(Mrs. Robins) of Gratton Farm,Highbray.

****

Susanna Tallyn(of Rye Park) died July 29,1929 at age 72. She is buried at Stoke Rivers.

Thomas Tallyn (1851) appears to have been the owner of a farm (Breara Manor) in Bratton Fleming. He later worked for the railroad at Bristol, England. His son, Thomas Brownscombe Tallyn is buried at Oceanview Burial Park, Vancouver, B.C.,Canada.

****

Barnstaple Registry of Deaths 1889 1st quarter(Jan.-Mar.)
Mary Brownscombe Tallyn age 0
This may be a daughter of Thomas Tallyn (1851).

---

1 Sources for this section include census and parish christening records of Stoke Rivers and Bratton Fleming and the Notes,& Recollections of W. Edwin Tallyn and Emory O. Forney (See Bibliography).

III. ANN TALLYN:[1]

Ann, the daughter of William R. and Mary Tallyn, was born about 1821 at Birch Farm of the Parish of Stoke Rivers. The 1841 census for Stoke Rivers lists Ann , under the household of her father, William (age 53). Her age is given as 20 .

Ann married James Tucker. The marriage is recorded in,Barnstaple Marriages, book of 1848, Vol. 10 page 85, 2nd quarter(April-June). The Tucker family surname is one of the oldest and most frequently associated with North Devon. Tooker (Tucker) is found in Domesday Book for Devonshire (Devrescira) 1085. James is no doubt related to the Tuckers of Stoke Rivers , neighbors of the Tallyns at Birch.

The 1851 census for Stoke Rivers show Ann and James Tucker on the farm at Birch. The family is listed as follows:

Birch	James Tucker	head	age 30	150 acres	B.Stoke Rivers
	(w) Ann	wife	30	"	"
	(s) John	son	2	"	"
	(s)James	son	1	"	"

The 1861 census for Stoke Rivers lists the family at Birch. Children born since the previous census include: William age 9, George age 7, Elizabeth age 6 and Ellen age 5.

Ann Tucker died, February 26,1871 at age 49. The 1871 census for Stoke Rivers taken shortly after her death reflects the household at the time. *********

Birch	James Tucker widower	age 49	Farmer 220 Acres	B. Stoke Rivers
	(s)(John	22	Farming	" "
	(s) William	16	"	" "
	(d) Elizabeth	15	Scholar	" "
	(d) Ellen T.	13	"	" "

Also listed under the household of James Tucker is:

Mary White	55	Nurse	Tentishoe
Thomas Pickard	17	Servant	Bratton Fleming
James Gore	13	Servant	Barnstaple

****

It is important to note that James(b. 1850) and George Tucker (1854) are not listed along with the other members of the family.
****

A Stoke Rivers Census Record of Interest:

	John Tucker	head	age 50 (275 acres)	B. Goodleigh
	Jane	63		Loxhore
1851 Census	John	24		Goodleigh
	Elizabeth	21		"

---

1 Sources used in this section include:1841,1851,1861 and 1871 census for Stoke Rivers, Barnstaple Marriages (Somerset Index) and death notice for Ann (Tallyn) Tucker of Stoke Rivers.

IV. ELIZABETH TALLYN:[1]

Elizabeth, the daughter of William R. and Mary Tallyn, was born around 1832 on the family farm at Birch of the Parish of Stoke Rivers. She appears, under the household of her father, on the 1841 census for Stoke Rivers. Her age is given as 9.   Unfortunately there is little additional information concerning Elizabeth. At some point in time she married a Mr. Hill. At the time of her brother's death (John Tallyn died 1902)Elizabeth was residing at Alcester (Warwick Co.), England.

****

V. GEORGE TALLYN:

Neither the year nor birth order is known for George. George and his brothers, Anthony and Joseph do not appear along with other members of the family on the 1841 census for Stoke Rivers. This seems to indicate he was similar to them in age or older. If George had been born after his sister, Elizabeth (1832) then the oldest he could have been in 1841 is about 8. It seems unlikely for him to have left the family domicile at such a young age. George may have been born during a 3-year interval between the births of Anthony (1823) and Mary (1826) or a similar interval   between Mary (1826) and Joseph (1829).

The obituary of John Tallyn, George's brother, indicates George Tallyn of Birch Farm died prior to John (May 14, 1902). The 1841 Census shows his father, William R. Tallyn at Birch. Ann(Tallyn) and James resided there between 1851 and 1871.   Ann Tallyn died in 1871. George may have resided at Birch at some point after 1871.

****

Ten children were born to William R. and Mary Tallyn of Stoke Rivers. Six of their ten children remained in England including: William (1815), John (1818), Ann (1821), Mary(1826),Elizabeth & George. Mary Tallyn married Thomas Ridd and they made their home at Southcott of Bratton Fleming. Mary died around 1864 and shortly after most of the family left England to settle in Jo Daviess County, Illinois. To facilitate matters data,for Mary (Tallyn) and Thomas Ridd and their descendants ,is presented in the following section,(Part II) Children and Descendants who Settled in America. This section includes Mary's descendants along with those of her brothers: James (1816), Thomas (1820), Anthony (1823) and Joseph Tallyn (1829).

---

[1]
Sources utilized in this section include the 1841, 1851, 1861 and 1871 census for Stoke Rivers and Bratton Fleming. and the 1902 obituary notice of John Tallyn (1818).

PART III Section B

(Those Descendants Who Settled in America)

CHILDREN AND DESCENDANTS OF WILLIAM R. AND MARY TALLYN
OF
STOKE RIVERS
DEVON ENGLAND

****

1

I. JAMES TALLYN:

James was the second child born to William R. and Mary Tallyn.
He was born in Bratton Fleming. Parish records there show he was
christened, November 10, 1816. Shortly after he was born the family
removed to Birch of the Parish of Stoke Rivers where James grew to
manhood. The 1841 census for Stoke Rivers shows James (age 24)
living at home and helping on the family farm.

Around 1845 he left his native Devon for America. He settled
in Jubilee of Jubilee Township of Peoria County Illinois. There
is but a slender store of information concerning James upon his
arrival in America. There is evidence that he made the trip to
America in the company of the Bradley family of Devon, who also
settled at Jubilee of Peoria County.

James was married. It is likely he and his bride met and wel-
comed Thomas R. and Elizabeth (Fry) Tallyn(his brother and sister-
in-law) upon their arrival in Peoria in 1847. James does not
appear on the 1850 US Census for Peoria County. One source notes
he died after a sudden and brief illness. This would seem to place
his death between 1847 and 1850. His wife's name is unknown and
he left no descendants. James was the first burial in the Jubilee
Cemetery. No stone was ever erected to mark the site of his
grave.

********* *****

The following entry is of interest. It _may_ refer to the
marriage of James Tallyn of this sketch.

<u>Barnstaple Marriages:</u>   , Vol 2, page 72, 1st. quarter (Jan.-Mar.)
1845.
(Married) James Tallyn

****

---

1 Sources for this section include the 1841 census for Stoke Rivers,
Bratton Fleming Christening Records, 1850 US Census for Peoria
County, Illinois and the <u>Notes, Recollections and Memorabilia</u> ,
<u>1979</u>:of Emory O. Forney of Minonk, Illinois.

II THOMAS R. TALLYN (1820-1876):

Thomas R. Tallyn[2] was born March 14,1820.He grew to manhood on the
family farm at Birch (Birch Farm) of Stoke Rivers. In March of 1847, near
his 27th birthday, Thomas married Elizabeth Fry. Their marriage is recorded in, Barnstaple Marriages, Vol. 10 p. 61, 1847, 1st quarter.
Elizabeth was born in February of 1826. She was the daughter of Thomas
and Betsy (Snell) Fry of the Parish of Swimbridge of Devon, England.
(Additional data for the Fry and Snell families is presented in the
Appendices)

Shortly after their marriage Thomas and Elizabeth sailed for
America. The crossing took seven weeks. Their destination was Peoria
Co.,Illinois. On their arrival they were met by James Tallyn, an old-
er brother to Thomas,who had come to America in 1845.

Like his brother, Thomas came to America to follow his interest in farming. Thomas and Elizabeth first settled in Rosefield Twp.
of the County, where they rented and operated a farm. Their two year
stay in the township was marked by the births of sons, William W. and
Thomas F. Tallyn.

During this period they were joined by relatives and friends
from England, who like themselves, had left their native homeland for
the promise of a better future in America. Around November of 1848
they were joined by Anthony and Susanna (Lee) Tallyn. The Fall of 1850
marked the arrival of Joseph Tallyn. Elizabeth's sister, Phoebe Ann,
and husband, John Ford,also arrived in 1850. Other friends and relatives,arriving around this time,included individuals of the Fry,
Lee, Huxtable and Harding families.

In 1851 Thomas and his brother-in-law, John Ford, purchased a
quarter section of prairie land in Section 32 of nearby Radnor Twp.
of Peoria County. Thomas, like John Ford, may have earned a portion
of the purchase price by helping shear 3,500 head of sheep belonging
to Bishop Chase[3] The task of clearing, breaking and cultivating the
land required much time and effort by both men. In time each developed
separate but adjoining farms of their own. (By 1900 John Ford had acquired 400 acres.)

Thomas continued to expand and improve his farm throughout his
lifetime. He was noted in the township for his work and interest in
expanding agriculture in the area. His concern for education was
evidenced in his service as a School Director for the township ,a
post he held for several years. Thomas and Elizabeth were charter
members of the Kickapoo Baptist Church, which, along with others,they
helped organize (March 28, 1851).

One of the earliest records for the family of Thomas and
Elizabeth (in America)stems from the 1850 US Census for Peoria Co.,Ill.

Tallyer, Thomas	age 30	Farmer	Born: England
(w) Elizabeth	25	Keeping House	" "
(s) William	1	_____	" Illinois

******

The mis-spelling of names on census returns was not uncommon.
The family of Anthony Tallyn is shown residing nearby. He appears
as Anthony Fallyn . John Ford is also shown residing nearby.

---

1 Ella Tibbetts was a major contributor to this section.
2 The R may have stood for Richard.
3 Bishop Chase came to the County in 1836.He was a stockman,landowner and
  founder of Jubilee College.

The farm where Thomas and Elizabeth lived out their lives contained a large comfortable and substantial home. Nearby grew a marvelous grove of 300 Walnut trees. [1] It was amid this pleasant rural setting that their children played, worked and grew to adulthood.

On August 5, 1876, Thomas R. Tallyn fell from a stack of grain. [2] His injuries proved fatal. His death occurred nine days later on August 14, 1876. His untimely death at age 56, was a tragic loss to his family, friends and community. Elizabeth continued to live out her years on the farm. Elizabeth (Fry) Tallyn died, January 25, 1901, approximately one month from her 75th birthday. Thomas and Elizabeth are buried in Jubilee Cemetery (Radnor Twp.) Peoria Co., Illinois. Eight children were born to the marriage. One child died, un-named, in infancy. Their surviving 7 children include: (1) William W., (2) Thomas F., (3) Elizabeth, (4) Frank H., (5) Lucy P., (6) John A., and Mary B. Tallyn.

THE CHILDREN AND DESCENDANTS OF THOMAS R. AND ELIZABETH (FRY) TALLYN
****

1. WILLIAM W. TALLYN: (1849-1909)

William was born in June of 1849. He was born in Rosefield Twp. of Peoria County, Illinois but spent much of his youth growing up in Radnor Twp. the site of the Tallyn homestead. Around 1878, William married Louisa Fry. Louisa was the daughter of Abraham and Agnes (Lee) Fry. (See Appendices for additional data on the Fry and Lee Families.) Louisa was born at Stoke Rivers Devon, England, in March of 1857.

The 1900 US Census for Peoria (Kickapoo Twp) Co., Illinois lists the family as follows:

Tallyn, William W.	age 50	June 1849	Farm Laborer	B. Illinois
(w) Louisa	43	Mar. 1857	_____	B. England
(s) Aubrey W.	2	Nov. 1897	_____	B. Illinois
Frank H.	45	May. 1855	(Brother to Wm)	"

Other census entries indicate William and Louisa had been married 22 years. It also shows that four children were born to the marriage. At the time of the census (1900), three of the four are living. There is no data for this child indicating it may have died in infancy.

The 1880 US Census shows William and Louisa first made their home in Woodford (Clayton Twp) Co., Illinois. On this census the family appears as follows:

Tallyn William W.	age 30	Farmer	B. Illinois
(w) Louisa	23	Keeping House	B. England
(s) Thomas	1	_____	B. Illinois
Abraham Fry (widower) (father-in-law)	69	part-time-work	B. England

---

1   Thomas F. Tallyn, the son of Thomas and Elizabeth, later dedicated the grove as a natural monument to the first pioneers of Peoria Co.

2   The notes of Emory O. Forney indicate the stack may have been oat bundles to be thrashed.

William W. Tallyn died in 1909. Louisa (Fry) Tallyn died,
January 30, 1923 at age 66. Louisa is buried in the Springdale Cemetery
of Peoria Co.,Illinois. Their surviving children include: Thomas,
Edith and Aubrey Tallyn.

A. Thomas Tallyn: Thomas was born, January 1879 in Woodford
Co.,Illinois. Late in 1880 the family removed to Radnor Twp.
of Peoria County, Illinois, where Thomas grew to manhood. The
1900 US Census for Peoria Co., lists Thomas (age 21) working
as a farm laborer on the farm of his uncle, John A. Tallyn.
Thomas died at age 29 (around 1908). There is some indication
he worked as a streetcar driver for Peoria Heights, Illinois.

B. Edith A. Tallyn: Edith was born in Kickapoo Twp. of Peoria
Co.,Illinois. The 1900 U.S. Census for Peoria County lists
Edith, age 19, under the household of Robert Fry and working
as a house servant. Edith was born December 10, 1880. She
married Amos Gough. There is little additional data for the
the family. Her obituary notice says she was 72 at the time
of death indicating she died in late 1952 or early 1953.This
notice states she was affiliated with the Peoria Heights Congregational Church, Four children were born to the marriage.Two
children, a son and daughter, preceded her in death. She was
survived by two sons and seven grandchildren. The children of
Edith and Amos Gough included: Robert, Thomas, John and Dorothy
Gough. Around 1952 Robert made his home in San Francisco,Calif.
and Thomas , Los Angeles, Calif.

C. Aubrey W. Tallyn: Aubrey was born in Peoria Counity, Illinois,
November 1, 1897. He appears under the household of his father,
William W. Tallyn, on the 1900 US Census for Peoria County. His
age is given as 2 . On July 23, 1921 , Aubrey married Doris D.
Campbell. Around 1929 he went to work for the Caterpillar Tractor
Co. of Peoria.He worked there 33 years before retiring, December
1, 1962. He was active in the Peoria Heights Congregational
Church and , at the time of death,its oldest member in terms of
membership. He belonged to the Caterpillar Retirees Club. He
lived most of his life in Peoria Heights. At the time of death
he was age 74.His widow survived him. Aubrey W. Tallyn is buried
in the Swan Lake Memorial Gardens of Peoria County. (No Children)

****

2. Thomas Frederick Tallyn: (1851-1946)

Thomas, the son of Thomas and Elizabeth (Fry) Tallyn, was born
in Rosefield Twp. of Peoria Co.,Illinois, March 5, 1851. In April of 1851
the family removed to Sec. 32 of Radnor Twp. of the County. Thomas grew
to manhood on the Tallyn homestead in Radnor Township. He obtained his
education at the nearby Tucker School.
On May 21, 1892, in Peoria County, Thomas married, Minnie
Rockwell. She was born in Aviesford of Kent County, England, May 17,1865,
One sources notes her family line is descended from the biblical,Ruth.
and John Alden of The Mayflower fame. Minnie was one of at least four
children. The family came to the United States in 1866. Minnie was two
years old when her mother died. She was raised in the home of Cyrus and
Fanny Tucker. The 1880 US Census for Peoria County lists her under the

household of Cyrus Tucker as follows:

Tucker, Cirus	age 71	Farmer	B. Mass.
(w) Fanny	57	Keeping House	Penn
(s) George	18	Farming	Illinois
Minnie Rockwell	15	(adopted)	England

****

Around 1881, Thomas purchased a farm in Radnor Township. In time he acquired other valuable acreage which included 40 acres of the original Tallyn-Ford homestead and 80 acres of the original Bishop Chase quarter of the township. Thomas was a member of the Baptist Church of Kickapoo, Illinois. At the time of death (1946) he was the last charter member of the Radnor Grange (organized:1874). He served as a School Director for the township. Thomas retired from farming and between 1923-46 he made his home in Peoria.

Thomas Frederick Tallyn died, March 4, 1946 at the home of his daughter, Ella (Tallyn) Tibbetts of Peoria.. He died just one day away from his 95th birthday. Minnie (Rockwell) Tallyn died, June 10, 1918, at age 52. She had been ill with measles and pneumonia for a brief period before her death. Thomas and Minnie are both buried in the Brimfield Cemetery at Brimfield, Illinois. Five children were born to the marriage.

The 1900 U.S. Census for Radnor Twp. of Peoria County, Illinois lists the family as follows:

Tallyn, Thomas F. age 49 b. Mar. 1851 Married 8yrs Farmer B. Ill.
(w) Minnie   35   May   1865 (To U.S. in 1866)   B. Eng.
(s) Clarence R.   7   Apr. 1893   B. Ill.
(d) Ella M.   3   Mar. 1897   B. "
(s) Everett T. (7 months) Oct. 1899   B. "

****

Not shown is Anna Adelia Tallyn, who was born later in 1902 and an infant son who died shortly after birth. He's buried, Brimfield Cemetery of Peoria County.

A. Clarence Rockwell Tallyn: Clarence was born, April 13, 1893 in Radnor Twp. of Peoria County. Clarence, a single man, spent his youth on the family farm......where he grew to adulthood. He was a gentle good natured man who enjoyed photography. His latter years were spent as a client of the State Hospital at Peoria. Clarence R. Tallyn died, November 14, 1967 at age 74. He is buried in Brimfield Cemetery at Brimfield, Illinois.

B. Ella May Tallyn: Ella was born, March 4, 1897. On November 7, 1918 , in Peoria County, she married, Ralph C. Tibbetts. Ralph, the son of Clyde and Cora (Jones) Tibbetts, was born in Averyville, September 21, 1897. Between 1925-57 (32 years) the family made their home in Prospect Heights, Ill. Around 1957 they moved to Rural Route Number One of Edwards, Illinois. About 1928 Ralph went to work for the Pabst Brewing Co. He worked in shipping until his retirement in 1963. He was a member of

---

* Cyrus Tucker was born, July 19,1809 in Plymouth, Mass. His first wife, Abigal T.A. Shaw died in 1846. On September 13, 1857 he married Fanny Keim who was born in Pennsylvania, May 19,1823.

Quarter Century Club of Pabst and a 40 year member of Grandview
Lodge 112 (AF and AM). Ralph C. Tibbetts died, June 23, 1968
at age 70. He is buried in Parkview Cemetery of Peoria Co.,Ill.
Ella (Tallyn) continues to make her home at R.R. #1, Edwards,
Illinois.

Ella is a 1914 graduate of the Tucker School. She is a 60
year member of the Peoria Heights Congregational Church and a
member of Women's Fellowship, WW Club and Radnor Grange. Her
hobbies include, reading, embroidering, sewing, flowers, travel,
playing the piano and genealogy. The children of Ralph and
Ella M. (Tallyn) Tibbetts include:

1. <u>Robert Ralph Tibbetts</u>:   Robert was born, May 23, 1922.
He was first married to Iva Hendrickson. (1 child)

       <u>Richard Allan Tibbetts</u>:   B. January 30, 1949

Robert's second marriage was to Beverly Stout. They were
married, August 17,1957. (1 child)

       <u>Daniel Robert Tibbetts</u>:   B. May 19, 1958

<u>Robert R. Tibbetts</u> is a 1941 graduate of Woodruff High School.
He served in the US Navy (1942-1945) during WW II, where he
obtained the rank of CPO 3rd class. He was active in the Normandy
Invasion and the Battle for Omaha Beach. He served aboard the
Destroyer, USS Thompson where met several notables including,
Generals Eisenhower, De Gaulle, Montgomery and Adm. King.
More recently he has been with the Acme Furnace Co. this
past <u>34</u> years as a sheetmetal worker. He is a member of De-
Molays and a Past Comander of Dunlap American Legion Post.
He enjoys camping, fishing, cards, gardening, bowling and play-
ing the violin.
<u>Beverly (Stout) Tibbetts</u>: Beverly is a graduate of Vista Grade
School (#7) and attended high school in Independence, Iowa.She
worked for the Caterpillar Tractor Co. for <u>21</u> years. She is a
Past President of the American Legion Aux. and member of the Catepillar Retirees Club. Her hobbies and interests include sewing,
embroidering, rug hooking, reading, camping, fishing and bowling.
<u>Daniel R. Tibbetts</u>: Daniel attended Wilder-Waite Elementary School
and is a 1977 graduate of Dunlap High School. He is presently in
the US Navy which he joined, July 29, 1977. His basic training was
completed at the US Naval Training Center at Great Lakes, Ill.
His tour of duty has included the carrier USS Ranger and presently the USS Howard Gilmore stationed at the Island of Sardinia
 Italy. Hull Technician, Daniel Tibbetts , enjoys fishing, biking,
and bowling.
****

2. <u>Virginia May Tibbetts</u>:   Virginia was born in Peoria Co.,
Illinois, October 12,1924. She married (1st) Robert Sims. No
children were born to the marriage. On January 3, 1955 she
married (2nd) William Messer. William, the son of Adam and Grace
(Dickeson) Messer, was born , January 18, 1922 in Tazewell Co.,
Illinois. William Messer died, June 10,1961. He is buried in
Parkview Cemetery of Peoria County. (2 children)

A. **Sheryl Diane Messer:** Sheryl was born in Peoria (Peoria Co), Illinois, October 30, 1956. She is a 1974 graduate of Dunlap High School. She is working as an auditor for Bergner's Dept. Stores Distribution Center of downstate Illinois. She is an active member of the Peoria Heights Congregational Church. In high school she was active in several music groups, drama, 4H, FFA, Pep and Pom-Pom organizations. Her hobbies and interests include Dirt Biking in her 4 wheel drive Bronco, horseback riding, bowling, pool, needlepoint, travel, ceramics and playing the organ.

B. **Joy Ann Messer:** Joy was born, February 4, 1959 in Peoria (Peoria Co.), Illinois. She graduated from Dunlap High School in 1977. She is employed as a private secretary at the State of Illinois Administrative Service. She is a member of the Peoria Heights Congregational Church. She is a former Brownie and Girl Scout. Her high school activities included 4H, Business Club, Echo Staff, candlemaking and knitting. She enjoys horseback riding, bowling, dirt biking and ceramics. She has a AKC registered Dalmatian. She hopes one day to be a veterinarian.

Mrs. William (Virginia) Messer is currently with Bergner's Dept. Stores and Distribution Center. She is a member of Peoria Heights Congregational Church. She attended Woodruff High School and Liberty Beauty School. Her past work experience has involved owning and operating the La Petite Beauty Salon. At Methodist Hospital she worked in Special Diets and at Proctor Hospital, the Maternity Ward. During WW II she worked on the bottle and can line at the Pabst Brewing Company. Her leisure time activities include bowling, flowers, horseback riding, golf, needlepoint, travel, reading and ceramics.

****

C. **Everett Thomas Tallyn:** Everett, the son of Thomas F. and Minnie (Rockwell) Tallyn, was born in Peoria County, Illinois, October 10, 1899. On May 21, 1920, in Peoria, he married Hazel Bertha Martin. Hazel, the daughter of Edward and Anna (Berg) Martin, was born at Dunlap of Peoria County, February 25, 1904. Everett was with the Caterpillar Tractor Co. of Peoria. He was affiliated with the Grace Presbyterian Church of Peoria. Hazel was a member of the Dunlap Methodist Church.

Hazel B. (Martin) Tallyn died, December 7, 1940 (age 36) at the family home at R.R. # 1 Edwards, Illinois. Everett Thomas Tallyn died, December 9, 1965 at age 66. Both are buried in Prospect Cemetery at Dunlap. Eight children were born to the marriage: (1) Clifford E., (2) Betty M., (3) Dorothy C., (4) Helen I., (5) James E., (6) Mary Louise, (7) Donald T. & (8) Hazel B. Tallyn.

1. **Clifford Eugene Tallyn:** Clifford was (B) July 21, 1921. He died, at home, (Edwards, Ill.) September 3, 1928 at age 7. He is buried in Prospect Cemetery, Dunlap, Ill.

2. **Betty Mae Tallyn:** Betty was born, September 16, 1923. On December 21, 1940, she married Keith Ross. Betty (Tallyn) Ross died, February 24, 1979 at Lansing, Michigan. 1 child

22

3. Dorothy Carrol Tallyn: Dorothy, the daughter of Everett T.
and Hazel B. (Martin) Tallyn, was born December 25, 1925. She grew up
and obtained her education in Peoria County, Illinois.
   Around 1941-42, in Peoria County, Dorothy married Thomas Williams.
The August 2, 1944 edition of the Peoria Star notes that Lt. Thomas
Williams (USAF), bombardier, was missing in action over Austria since
July 17, 1944. It goes on to indicate that Thomas enlisted in June of
1942. He went through training at Santa Ana, California. He served as
an instructor in California and Arizona prior to being sent overseas.
   Thomas was a graduate of Dunlap High School of Peoria County, Ill.
His mother, Mrs. Edna Williams, is listed as one notified by the War
Department.
   Dorothy and Thomas made their home in Peoria County. One child
was born to the marriage.

   a. Thomas LeRoy Williams: Thomas was born May 19,1943.
   He was verly likely born in Peoria or Dunlap of Peoria Co.,
   Illinois.

   There is little additional data for the family. A 1965 obituary
notice for Everett T. Tallyn indicates Dorothy (Tallyn) Williams
made her home in San Francisco, California.

******

4. Helen Irene Tallyn: Helen was born, January 14, 1927 . Helen was
   twice married. Her first was to E. Hayes. One child, Patrica Anne,
   was born to the marriage. She later married (2nd) Robert Wilson.
   Robert was born in Peoria (Peoria Co.), Illinois, October 8, 1923.
   He is the son of Cecil and Mildred (Witherell) Wilson. Helen and
   Robert were married, March 30, 1946. Two children were born to
   the marriage: Robert Steven and Monte Lee Wilson.

   A. Patrica Anne Hayes: Patrica was born, May 24, 1944.
      She completed two years of collage. She presently works
      for the School Board in Houston, Texas. Earlier,at Peoria,
      she worked as a secretary for Woodruff High School and
      Assistant to the Dean of Boys. Her interests include art
      and interior design.
         On November 21, 1964, Patrica married, Edward Gleason.
      (2 children)
            1. Tina Renee Gleason: (B) January 7, 1966
            2. Douglas Edward Gleason: (B) Nov. 28, 1968.

      Patrica subsequently married (2nd), in 1979, Theodore
      Evans.

   B.Robert Steven Wilson: Robert was born December 13, 1947.
     Hes completed 2 years of college. He served during the
     Vietnam War (Preventive Medicine). He is presently with
     Caterpillar Tractor Co.(Art Depart).His interests include

23

art and golf. On June 10, 1967, Robert married, Linda
Lee Pieper. (2 children)

    1. <u>Gregory Robert Wilson</u>:   (B) Jan.   18, 1970

    2. <u>Jennifer Lynn Wilson</u>:   (B) March   16, 1972

<u>Monte Lee Wilson</u>: Monte was born, January 22, 1957. He
presently works as a mechanic for a foreign car company. In
high school he played football. A boy scout, his interests
include guitar, piano, art and <u>girls</u>. He is a Formula Race
Car trophy winner.

               ****

5. <u>James Edward Tallyn</u>:   James was born, June 21, 1930, Edwards,
Illinois. He attended Tucker Grade School and Dunlap High. He
served in the US Army (1951-53) Signal Corp, as a Teletype Operator,
in Fulda, Germany. He is a part-time carpenter and has 25 years of
service with Caterpillar Tractor Co. as a Machinist. His leisure
activities include, woodwork, gardening, camping, fishing and travel.
    On April 24, 1949, James married, Winona Rosenow. She is the
daughter of Everett H. and Hazel E. (King) Rosenow. Winona was born,
November 28, 1929, Kewanee, Kansas. She attended Roosevelt Jr. High
and Toulon High School. She is a member of the Prospect Methodist
Church. Her interests include gardening, flowers, camping, fishing
and travel. Four children, (1) <u>Betty</u>, (2)<u>Joette</u>,(3)<u>James</u> and (4)
<u>Janine</u> Tallyn were born to the marriage. All were born in Peoria
(Peoria Co.), Illinois.

    1. <u>Betty JoLona Tallyn</u>:   (B)March 13, 1956
    Betty is a graduate of Princeville Elementary and High
    Schools. On September 3, 1977, she married Larry Kerns.
    (child)

        <u>Chad James Kerns</u>:   (B) May 20,1978

    2. <u>Joette Louise Tallyn</u>:   (B) January 10, 1958
    She is a graduate of Princeville grade and high schools.
    On May 20, 1977, Joette married Larry Seidell. (1 child)
        <u>Chirstopher James Seidell</u>: (B) July 24, 1978

    3. <u>James Kevin Tallyn</u>:   (B) December 8, 1960
    James is a graduate of Princeville grade and high schools.
    He played football (2yrs) in high school and also two years
    in Little League. His interests include reading and stereo-
    electronics.

    4. <u>Janine Marie Tallyn</u>:   (B) February 25, 1962
    Janine is a graduate of Princeville Grade School. She has
    been a member of the 4H Club(5 years) winning blue ribbons
    for her rabbits and goats. Her hobbies include camping
    and hiking.

               ****

6. Mary Louise Tallyn: Mary was born, October 3, 1932, at Dunlap
(Peoria Co.), Illinois. On October 29. 1954, she married, Delman White.
They were married at Bloomington, Illinois. Delman, the son of Roy and
Mary White, was born, July 26, 1934 at Danvers, Illinois. (1 child)

   Sharon Louise White: Sharon was born,September 25, 1954 at
   Peoria, Illinois. She married Roger Stegeman. (2 children)

      a. Roger Stegeman: (B) April 25, 1974 Hannibal, Missouri

      b. Ryan Stegeman: (B) Sept. 9, 1977   "   "

                        ****

   7. Donald Thomas Tallyn: Donald was born, September 12, 1935,(Rural)
Edwards (Peoria Co.), Illinois. Don attended Dewey Grade School of
Rural Dunlap, Roosevelt Junior High and Woodruff High School. He is
presently a Manager (Hardware) at Sears Roebuck. He is affiliated with
the St. Thomas Church. He is a member of Astronomical Society, Academy
of Science and Lakeview Museum. His interests include bowling,sports,
and stained glass making.
   At St. Philomena Church of Peoria, he married, August 4, 1954, Gwen
Ruhland. She is the daughter of Albert Henry and Dorothy Mildred(Lardy)
Ruhland. Gwen was born, August 28, 1938,Paynesville, Minnesota.
   Gwen attended elementary schools in Minnesota, Iowa and Illinois.
She attended, The Academy of Our Lady at Peoria, Illinois. She is a
homemaker and artist. She gives demonstrations for the ancient craft
of Wheat Weaving. She also sells and exhibits the designs. She is a
member of St. Thomas Church, Astronomical Society, Academy of Science,
Lakeview Museum, Fine Arts Society, Symphony Guild and Picture Lady
Volunteer. Her interests include the design of decor wall hangings
clothing, etc. and reading,music, art astronomy and quilting.
   Don and Gwen have five children: (1)Stephen A., (2)Cyndi S.,(3)
Kristen L., (4) Scott M., and Karen C. Tallyn. All were born in Peoria
(Peoria Co.), Illinois.

   A.Stephen Anthony Tallyn: B. May 3, 1955
     Steve attended St Mary's and St Patricks Grade Schools. and
     Bergan and Peoria Heights High Schools. He has an Architectural
     Construction Degree from I.C.C.College. He is presently, Asst.
     Manager at Getz Smoke and Fire Alarm Systems Co. His interests
     include architecture, golf, baseball and stained glass.
     On May 29, 1977, Steve married, Margaret Mitchell.

   B. Cynthia Spring Tallyn: B. July 9, 1956   Cyndi is a
     graduate of I.C.C. College. Her elementary and secondary
     studies were completed at St. Mary's and St. Patricks Grade
     Schools and Bergan High School. She is a secretary. Her
     leisure activies include, reading, sewing and quilting.
     On June 30, 1979, Cyndi married, Robert True.

   C. Kristen Lynn Tallyn: B. November 3, 1957   Kris went
     to St. Mary's, St. Patricks and Gardner Grade Schools. She
     is a graduate of Bergan High School. At Illinois State
      University at Normal, she obtained a degree in Music and
     Music Therapy. She enjoys reading, needlepoint and playing
     the piano.
                          25

D. Scott Michael Tallyn: Scott was born February 10, 1960. He attended St. Marys, St. Patricks and Gardner elementary schools. He is a graduate of Bergan High School. Scott also attended Southern Illinois State University at Carbondale, Ill. His hobbies include astronomy and photography.

E. Karen Camille Tallyn: Karen was born April 23, 1968. She attended Gardner, St. Thomas and Father Sweeney grade schools. She is a Jr. Girl Scout and enjoys drama, reading, sewing, cooking, music, ballet, dancing and kickball.

****

8. Hazel Bertha Tallyn:

Hazel is the 8th and last child born to Everett T. and Hazel B. Tallyn. She was born in Peoria County, Illinois December 7, 1940. It is of interest to note that Hazel's date of birth is the same as her mother's date of death.
At the time of her mother's death Hazel was unnamed. It is more than a concidence that she was named after her mother, Hazel Bertha (Martin) Tallyn.
Around 1960 Hazel married Joe Dillman. The 1965 obituary notice for Everett T. Tallyn indicates the family resided in St. Petersberg, Florida. Three children were known to have been born to the marriage. The December 1965 obituary for Everett T. Thomas notes that he was survived by 17 grandchildren indicating the three children of Hazel and Joe Dillman were born prior to December of 1965. They may have been born in Florida.

A. Cynthia Dillman:

B. David Dillman:

C. Mark Dillman:

****

This concludes the listing of the children and descendants of Everett Thomas Tallyn and Hazel Bertha Martin.

The author is indebted to Ella (Tallyn) Tibbetts for making her notes and records for the family available for use in this document.

D. Anna Adelia Tallyn: Anna, of Thomas and Minnie (Rockwell)
Tallyn, was born, February 27, 1902. On October 29, 1921, Anna
married Walter B. Martin. Walter was born, January 22, 1902.(Walter
was probably the son of Edward and Anna (Berg) Martin of Dunlap, Ill.)
Anna died, August 21, 1929 (age 27) . She is buried in Brimfield
Cemetery , Brimfield (Peoria Co.),Illinois. Walter B. Martain died,
May of 1966, Kansas City   2 children

1. Wilfred Walter Martin:He was born, March 23,1924 , Edwards,
   Illinois. Wil is a 1959 graduate of Tampa University. In
   1942 he joined the US Air Force. He took his basic training
   at Miami Beach. During his long and distinguished career
   Lt. Col. Martin flew a wide range of aircraft from prop to
   jet planes. His many tours of duty included stations in
   the US and overseas.At various times he served as training
   officer,squadron operations officer and assignments officer.
   He had over 5,000 hours of flying time.
         He completed a degree in Business Administration. After
   his retirement he went into business for himself as a business consultant. He was one of five Delaware delegates
   selected to attend a White House Conference on Small Business.
   His leisure activities center about his life long interest
   in barbershop singing. He is a member of S.P.E.B.S.Q.S.A.
         On July 12, 1947, in Bloomington, Illinois, Wil
   married, Betty R. Uhrie. Betty, the daughter of Raymond
   and Orva (Burton) Uhrie, was born, April 21, 1925. She
   obtained her education in the schools of Bloomington. She
   served as officer manager and partner in the family business,
   General Business Services, In., a Maryland based franchise
   operation. She was active in the Wesley United Methodist
   Church and a member of the Ladies Aux. of the First State
   Chorus. Betty (Uhrie) Martin died, August 14,1979 (age 54),
   at the Dover AF Base Hospital after a long illness. She is
   buried in Lakeside Cemetery, Dover, Md. Two children were
   born to the marriage.

   1. Josephine Martin: (B) January 1, 1949 Jody is a
      graduate of the U. of Delaware.Her degree is
      in music. She owns and operates a dog groom-
      ing business (5 yrs). She has show dogs and
      is well known in the East where they are shown.

   2. Ray Martin: (B) January 1, 1952   On December 28,
      1974, Ray married Rebecca Bogegrain. She is
      the daughter of the Rev. Walter and Patricia
      Bogegrain. Ray, a lawyer, works for the firm
      of Mueth and Erbuger of Denver, Colorado.
      Rebecca (Becky) is an executive in a con-
      struction firm.

2. Mildred Irene Martin: Mildred was born, July 13, 1926,
   Edwards (R.R. #1), Illinois. She married Frank Buhl.(1
   child)

   Mary Ann Buhl:

27

3. <u>ELIZABETH A. TALLYN:</u> (1853-1906)

Elizabeth, the daughter of Thomas R. and Elizabeth (Fry) Tallyn, was born in March of 1853, Peoria County, Illinois. She was lovingly called, "Aunt Lizzie" by many. She kept house for two different men and went by the last name of each, respectively, Lizzie Diamond and Lizzie Kennedy.

The <u>1900 US Cenus</u> for Peoria County (Radnor Twp), Illinois lists Elizabeth (age 45) under the household of her brother, John A. Tallyn. This record shows her divorced. Another source indicates she never married. Elizabeth A. Tallyn died in 1906 around age 52. She made her home at Prospect Heights, Illinois. She is very likely buried in Peoria County.

****

4. <u>FRANK H. TALLYN:</u> (1855-1922)

Frank, the son of Thomas R. and Elizabeth(Fry) Tallyn, was born in May of 1855, Peoria County (Radnor Twp), Illinois. Frank; a single man, traveled extensively in the US and particularly the West.

The <u>1880 U.S. Census</u> for Peoria County lists Frank, age 24, under the household of his brother, Thomas Frederick Tallyn. They are both listed as <u>single</u> and <u>farming</u>. The <u>1900 US Census</u> for the County,enumerates Frank under the household of William W. Tallyn and family of Kickapoo Township. William was Frank's oldest brother.

In 1910 Frank (age 55) is back living with his brother, Thomas F. Tallyn. Frank H. Tallyn died in 1922.(around age 67). He is very likely buried in Peorio County, Illinois.

****

5. <u>LUCY F. TALLYN: (1856-1886)</u>

Lucy, the daughter of Thomas R. and Elizabeth (Fry)Tallyn, was born, June 10, 1856, in Peoria Co., Illinois. Around 1879 she married, William Jones. He was the son of John and Anna Jones. They were both born in England around 1836. .William was born in Illinois around 1857.

The <u>1880 U.S. Census</u> for Radnor Twp. of Peoria County, Illinois, lists the family of William and Lucy (Tallyn) Jones, under the house-hold of William's father, John Jones.

Jones, John	age 44	Farmer	Born: England
(w) Anna	44	Keeping House	" "
(s) William	22	Farming	" Illinois
(w) Lucy	24	(son's wife)	" "
(s)Dwight	9 mo's.	(grandson)	" "

******

The farm of John Jones is shown as being located near the one owned by, Thomas Frederic Tallyn, Lucy's brother.

Lucy F. (Tallyn) Jones died, May 20, 1886, two months short of her 30th birthday. She is very likely buried in Peoria County, Ill. Four children were born to the marriage.

A. <u>Dwight Jones:</u>(1879-1937) Dwight was born, September 3, 1879 in Radnor Twp. of Peoria Co.,Ill.   On February 12, 1920, he married Hazel Hayward. The family made their home in Peoria where Dwight was a con-tractor. He was a member of the Alta Masonic Lodge, Peoria Consistory, A worthy patron of the Grandview Chapter of Eastern Star and a past noble grand of the Odd fellows.

Dwight Jones died in 1937 at age 58. He is buried in Parkview Cemetery of Peoria County. Two children were born to the marriage.

1. <u>Muri R. Jones:</u>

2. <u>Claire Jones:</u>

It is most likely, Muri and Claire were born in Peoria Co. In 1937 , at the time of their father's death, they made their home in Dunlap of the County.

2. <u>Augustus Jones:</u> The infant son of William and Lucy (Tallyn) Jones was born, January 13,1881. He died February 3, 1881.

3. <u>Raymond Jones:</u> Raymond was born, August 6, 1883. He married Edith Ford. Raymond died, May 9,1973, just three month prior to his 90th birthday. The family made their home at Peoria, Illinois. 1 child

a.<u>Helen Jones:</u>

4. <u>Myrtis Jones:</u> Myrtis, the daughter of William and Lucy (Tallyn) Jones, was born, November 28, 1881, Radnor Twp. of Peoria Co.,Illinois. On December 30, 1911, in Bloomington, Illinois, she married,John Henry Beverly. Myrtis was a member of Radnor Grange, the Worthwhile Club, Leisure Hour Sunday School Class and Peoria Heights Congregational Church.
Myrtis (Jones) Beverly died, Spetember 11, 1953 at age 71. She had been in poor health about a month prior to death. She is buried in Parkview Cemetery of Peoria Co. Her husband, John, survived her. (It appears that no children were born to the marriage.)

*****

6. <u>JOHN A. TALLYN:</u> (1859-1946)

John, the son of Thomas R. and Elizabeth (Fry) Tallyn, was born in Radnor Twp. of Peoria Co.,Illinois in September of 1859. The <u>1880 US Census</u> for Peoria County, lists John (age 20) under the household of his widowed mother (Elizabeth age 53). On January 27, 1897 John married, Bertha Lucy Challacombe. Bertha, the daughter of James and Lucy A. (Rogers) Challacombe, was born, November 17, 1870 Peoria County, Illinois. [1] John took over the Tallyn homestead founded by his father, Thomas R. Tallyn. He was an active member of the Radnor Grange for over 60 years.   John A. Tallyn died in the farm home where he had been born some 86 years earlier. He died, May 13,1946.
Bertha was active in the rural activities of Peoria Co. She was a 50 year member of Radnor Grange.She was affiliated with the Presbyterian Church of Alta and a member of the Leisure Hour Club. Bertha Lucy (Challacombe) Tallyn died, July 1950 at age 80. John and Bertha were buried in Springdale Cemetery of Peoria Co.,Illinois.

---

1 James was the son of Wm and Anna(Stevens) Challacombe. He was born in Devon, Eng.,Dec.25,1836. He came to the US in 1858. In 1868,James married (1st) Lucy A. Rogers of Devon, Eng. <u>Charles</u> and <u>Bertha</u> were born to the marriage. Lucy died in 1876. In 1876 James married (2nd) Sarah H. Rogers, a sister to Lucy. They had three children, <u>Archie</u>, <u>Bruce</u> and <u>Edna</u> Challacombe.

One child was born to the marriage of John and Bertha Tallyn.

     <u>Verna Mabel Tallyn</u>: Verna was born in Radnor Twp. of Peoria County, Illinois, in November of 1898. In Peoria, on March 16, 1920, Verna married Charles A. Haller. Charles, the son of George H. and Augusta (Patton) Haller, was born in Radnor Twp., November 25, 1893.[1]
    Verna was a member of the Presbyterian Church, Peoria Women's Club, Homemakers Extension, a past matron of Alpha Chapter, 256. O.E.S. and Radnor Grange. Verna Mable (Tallyn) Haller died, December 14, 1965 at age 67. (1 child)

     a. <u>Carol Haller</u>: (died in infancy)

Charles married (2nd) the former Mrs. Sadie(Predmore) Smith.[2] They were married, January 10, 1969. Charles retired from farming in 1963. He served as president, director and board member of various farm-related organizations. He was a member of Alta Lodge 748. AF&AM, Peoria Consistory, Scotish Rite: Mohammed Temple, Shrine and Alta Chapter, O.E.S.   Charles A. Haller died, April 8, 1976 at age 82. Both Charles and Verna are buried in Springdale Cemetery of Peoria Co.

****

7. <u>MARY B. TALLYN</u>: (1862-1942)

     Mary, the daughter of Thomas R. and Elizabeth (Fry) Tallyn, was born in Peoria County, July 10, 1862. The <u>1880 US Census</u> for the County lists Mary (age 17) under the household of her widowed mother,Elizabeth (age 53) and brother, John A. Tallyn (age 20). In 1890, Mary married William Jones. William,the son of John and Anna Jones, was first married to Mary's sister, Lucy F. (Tallyn) Jones. Mary B. (Tallyn) Jones died, December 29,1942 at age 80. She is buried in Parkview Cemetery of Peoria County. William Jones died in September of 1928.

****

     This concludes the enumeration of the children and descendants of Thomas R. and Elizabeth (Fry) Tallyn.....

---

1 His <u>middle</u> name was probably <u>Augusta</u>. George H. Haller was born in Cincinnati, Ohio, Jan. 20, 1850. George was the son of Conrad J. (1804-1855) and Christina (Koerner) Haller (1822-1899). Both were natives of Kittweil of Wurtemburg, Germany. Augusta (Patton) Haller, was born, Sept. 12,1859(Kickapoo Twp.), the daughter of J.B. and Harriet Patton. Augusta died, October 25, 1900.
2 Two sons, James and Milton Smith were born to this previous marriage.

III. ANTHONY TALLYN: (1823-1867)

Anthony Tallyn was born, July 20, 1823 at Birch (Birch Farm) of the Parish of Stoke Rivers, Devon, England. On Christmas Day, December 25, 1843, at age twenty, Anthony was baptised in the Brayford Baptist Church.

There is evidence Anthony spent a few years in America prior to returning to England to marry. On September 16, 1848, Anthony married Susanna Lee. A record of the marriage is contained in: Barnstaple Marriages, Vol. X , page 76, 3rd Quarter, 1848. Susanna, the daughter of Thomas and Mary Lee, was born, December 27, 1823, at Lower Davis Farm of Stoke Rivers. (See Lee Family in Appendix.)

Anthony and his bride set sail for America, October 21,1848. In America they settled (1st.) in Kickapoo of Peoria Co.,Illinois. The 1850 US Census for the County lists the family as follows:

Fallyn, Anthony	age 26	Sailor	B. England
(w) Susannah	26	Keeping House	England

****

The census taker appears to have had difficulty with the family surname. Emory O. Forney indicates his grandfather was a tailor and not a sailor. He recalls seeing his grandfather's large pressing irons.

The 1850 census does not list their son, James Tallyn, who was born in July of 1850, shortly after the census was taken. The census shows the family residing between the families of Thomas Tallyn and John Ford.

Anthony and Susanna were charter members of the Kickapoo Baptist Church which, along with others, they helped organize . Peoria County was the place of birth for their children: James, Anne Lee, Mary Marcia and Charles A. Tallyn.

In 1856, Anthony purchased some farm land in Woodford County, Illinois. In 1857, they moved to the County and settled on a farm near the present town of Benson (Clayton Twp.). It is doubtful the family ever forgot their first year in the county and the terrible night of May 13, 1858. It was the day of the first great storm of Woodford County and historian, Roy L. Moore provides the following account of that fateful event:

> ".....In Clayton Township Mrs. Susanna Tallyn had a thrilling experience, and a narrow escape from death.She still remembers with horror that terrible night with its dangers. Her husband was outside looking after the stock when the storm came up. They were also living in a house that was not completed, yet it was regarded perfectly safe. The storm destroyed the house and caught Mrs. Tallyn between the wall & the stove in such a manner that it was necessary to cut her clothing away before she could be removed. She and three small children were in the house together when the storm came, but as if by a miracle none of them were seriously injured. Mr. Tallyn, who was on the outside, was injured by having one of the out buildings fall on him."

From: History of Woodford County,by Roy L. Moore
Woodford Co. Republican, Publisher, Eureka, Ill. ,1910

The article fails to mention Susanna was six months pregnant with daughter, Caroline,at the time, which serves to heighten the drama of that unforgettable night.

Anthony and Susanna, along with others, were instrumental in found-ing (1859) the Clayton Baptist Church. The first services were held at the home of James and Fanny (Ridge) Huxtable. Anthony served as a church deacon for several years.

The 1860 US Census for Woodford County provides an early record of the family in the county.They are listed as follows:

Tallyn, Anthony	age 36	Farmer	B. England
(w) Susanna	35	Keeping House	England
(d) Ann	7	At Home	Illinois
(d) Mary	5	" "	"
(s) Charles	3	" "	"
(d) Catherine	1	" "	"

****

It is of interest to note that Caroline continues to be listed as Catherine until the 1880 census when she appears,correctly, as Carrie.

Anthony Tallyn died, March 9,1867 at age 43.* Two sons, James and John Franklin Tallyn preceeded him in death. This series of tragic losses is reflected in the 1870 US Census for Woodford County:

Tallyn, Susanna	age 46	widow	B. England
(d) Anne	17	At Home	Illinois
(d) Mary	15	" "	"
(s) Charles	13	" "	"
(d) Catherine	11	" "	"
(s) Freddy	6	" "	"

****

Susanna continued to make her home on the farm until 1883 when she moved to Benson. Susanna (Lee) Tallyn died at her Benson home, June 20,1912 at age 88. Prior to her death she had requested that the remains of Anthony and children, John Franklin and Mary Marcia be moved from the Old Clayton Cemetery to the New Clayton Cemetery of Woodford Co., the place of her interment. This request was fulfilled through the efforts of Gordon Tallyn, Daniel Davis, Charles Tallyn, John Fry and an uni-dentified Benson drayman.

The obituary for Susanna appeared in the Minonk Dispatch, June 27, 1912. It gives testimony to her Christian faith and character. A excerpt; from this tribute is presented below:

"....When but a young girl she united with the Baptist Church of Stoke Rivers, England and later transferred her membership by letter to the Baptist churches of Kickapoo, Clayton and Benson, Illinois, being a charter member of the two latter, whose support she was a liberal contributor......She lived a consistent christian life and was a true type of noble womanhood: Kind, loving and unselfish. Her end was as peaceful as her life had been, and she passed into that Great Beyond full of faith and hope in her eternal welfare. The memory of this sainted mother is a heritage worth having and the sweet influence of her beautiful life will stimulate those who knew her best. "She has fought a good fight, she has kept the faith, she has finished her course, "...........and her reward is sure."

****

---

* His death was attributed to consumption(pulmonary tuberculosis) aggra-vated by a fall involving runaway horses, a few days prior to his death.

Children And Descendants of Anthony and Susanna (Lee)
Tallyn:

****

I. JAMES RICHARD TALLYN: (1850-1851)
James was born in Kickapoo Peoria County, Illinois, July 22, 1850.
He died, July 3, 1851.

II. ANNE LEE TALLYN: (1852-1889)
     Anne was born in Kickapoo(Peoria Co.,Ill.) , August 25, 1852. She
married Joseph F. Pickard. Joseph was born in England around 1847. The
1880 US Census for Woodford County lists Joseph's occupation as carri-
age maker. Joseph and Anne made their home in Minonk, Illinois.
     Anne Lee (Tallyn) Pickard died, June 17, 1889 just two months prior
to her 37th birthday. She is buried in Minonk (Woodford Co.), Ill.
     In Bristol, New Hampshire, Joseph married (2nd) Katie M. Danforth
(1860-1950). They were married, December 2, 1890. Katie was most likely
the daughter of C.R. Danforth, a banker and notary public of Minonk.
Joseph Pickard was also a notary public for Woodford County. Joseph
died in 1916 around age 69. He is buried at Minonk. No children were
born to the second marriage. Three children were born to Anne(Tallyn)
and Joseph Pickard.

   A. Mabel M. Pickard:(1876-1893)   Mabel was born in Minonk in 1876.
      She died in 1893 (about age 17) and is most likely buried in Minonk
      (Woodford, Co.),Illinois. She left no descendants.

   B. Judson Tallyn Pickard: (1877-1952)   Judson was born in Minonk,
      December 16, 1877. Like his father, Judson was a notary public for
      Woodford County, Illinois. The 1900 US Census for Woodford County
      lists his occupation as: Cashier.
           On October 30, 1902, Judson married, Bertha Belle Herr. She
      was born in 1881.   2 children

         1. Chauncy Pickard: He was born in 1904. He died, 1905.

         2. Judson Eugene Pickard: Judson was married around 1942
         to Jayne Sherry Sheares.   1 child

               a. Joseph Pickard: Joseph was born around 1944.
               He makes his home in California.

      Bertha Belle (Herr) Pickard died in 1938 around age 57. Judson
      married (2nd) Margaret Walsh. No children were born of this
      marriage. Margaret (Walsh) Pickard died,around 1955 and is buried
      by her first husband.
           Judson Tallyn Pickard died, October 23,1952 two months prior
      to his 75th birthday. He is most likely buried in Minonk(Woodford
      Co.),Illinois.

   C. Fern Vera Pickard: (1889-   ) Fern was born in Minonk, May 6,
      1889. On December 2, 1920, she married, Thomas Donald Piche'.
      Thomas was born, August 4, 1885. They made their home in
      Homestead, Florida. Thomas died July 22, 1967. (Another source
      says July 17, 1967). He is very likely buried at Homestead.
      Fern is the first of several Tallyn descendants to attend and
      graduate from Shurtleff College of Alton, Illinois. 2 children

33

(1) Joseph and (2) Judson Piche': Joseph and Judson, twins, were born in Homestead, Florida, November 17, 1922. They were Co-Valedictorians of their class at Technical High School, Miami, Florida. Both served in the US Air Force during WW II.

Joseph Piche' 1st. Lt. Joe Piche', a fighter pilot, was shot down and killed over France, July 16(or 17), 1944. He left no descendants.

Judson Piche': Jud has been with National Airlines for the past 28 years. He was married but is now separated. Jud makes his home in South Miami, Florida. No Descendants

******

III. MARY MARCIA TALLYN: (1854-1895) [1]

Mary Marcia or Marcia as she was known, was born in Kickapoo Peoria Co.,Illinois, August 12, 1854. Around 1858 the family removed to Woodford County, Illinois, where she spent her youth and grew to adulthood. On October 10, 1878, in Benson, she married, Daniel Davis. Daniel, the son of James and Nancy (Highland) Davis, was born, April 16, 1851, Varna, Illinois. Daniel served as the first president of the Village Board of Benson, Constable and Railraod Station Agent.

Mary Marcia (Tallyn) Davis died, February 2, 1895 at age 40. She is buried in Clayton Twp. Cemetery. Daniel married (2nd) Eunice Kirby (1869-1950). No children were born to this marriage. Daniel Davis died in Miami, Florida, January 22, 1931. He is buried at Benson, Illinois. Two children were born to Mary Marcia(Tallyn) and Daniel Davis.

A. Bertha Myrtle Davis: (1881-1943)

Bertha was born in Benson, December 21, 1881. In Benson, on August 28, 1901, Bertha married, Frank Crichfield (b. March 24, 1870). Bertha Myrtle (Davis) Crichfield died in Springfield, Illinois, April 11, 1943 at age 62. She is buried at Springfield. Eight children were born to the marriage.

1. Pearl Kester Critchfield: B. October 11, 1902 Pearl married(5-28-1925) Harold Hensel. 2 children
   a. Daniel Hensel: B. 3-9-1936 D. 3-9-1936
   b. Ruth Elaine Hensel: B. April 11, 1937
      Ruth married (6-18-1955) Dale Carls   4 children
      1. Penny Carls: B. 3-26-1958
      2. Debby Carls: B. 2-20-1959
      3. Terry Carls: B. 11-19-1960
      4. Danny Carls: B. 9- 1-1964

2. Ruth Marcia Critchfield: B. November 15, 1903. She married (Sept. 1, 1925) Adam Cooper (b.   d. 11-11-1971) 1 child

   A. Maria Elaine Cooper: B. April 21, 1941   Maria married (Aug. 30, 1964) Paul Linus. 3 children
      1. Elaine Linus: B. 10-14-1968
      2. Connie Linus: B. 3-12-1971
      3. Nick Linus: B. 2-24-1972

---

1 This section is based on the notes of Vida G. (Davis) Davison.

3. Frances Joy Crichfield: B. Feb. 16,1905. She married
(7-20-1926) Glanville Camp (b.   d. 4-20-1974).
2 children

    1.William Howard Camp: B. 10-14-1928. He married
    (7-27-1957) Jerri Wind. 1 child

        a. Carol Camp: B. 10-4-1967

    2. Robert Daniels Camp: B.   2-16-1936
                           D.   5- 6-1942

4. Forrest Daniel Crichfield: B. Feb. 20,1907
                         D. Oct. 11,1939
Forrest married (5-3-1928) Dolly Epperley. 1 child
    1. Douglas Crichfield: B. 2-14-1930. Douglas 1st
     married Mary Lou Remington. 1 child
        a. Forest Douglas Crichfield: B. 5-10-1953
    Douglas then married (2nd) Bea. 1 child
        b. Michael Crichfield: B. 4- 1-1969

5.Vida Myrtle Crichfield: B. Feb. 4,1909
                     D. Aug. 2,1909

6.Merlyn Rupert Crichfield: B. Dec. 10,1910   He married
    (August 5, 1940) Mildred Joy . No children

7. John Howard Crichfield: B. Jan. 11,1912. John married
    (4-29-1931) Helen Windle. 3 children

    1. Judith Joy Crichfield: B. Oct. 15,1939. She married
    (12-1-1958) James Mullen.   2 children

        a. Michael Mullen: B. 9- 8-1959

        b. Tiffany Mullen: B. 8- 8-1970

    2.Elizabeth Ann Crichfield: B.July 25, 1943. She
     married (9-24-1962) Ronald Rouland.   4 children

        a.Randal Rouland: B.   4-18-1964
        b.Richard Rouland: B.   2-28-1966
        c.Robert Rouland: B.   1- 9-1968
        d.Ryan   Rouland: B.   6-26-1970

    3. Margaret Lynn Crichfield:B. Feb. 4, 1947. She
     married(July 11, 1965) Gary Heffelfinger. 1 child

        a. Gary James Heffelfinger: B. Feb. 20, 1967

8. Helen Eunice Crichfield: B. December 17, 1916.
                         D. November 2, 1971
    She first married Jack Cable. 1 child

    1. Jackie Joy Cable: B.Sept. 4, 1942 Jackie first
     married Mr. Lamanan. 1 child
        a.Stephanie Ann Lamanan:B. April 3, 1965

Jackie Joy (Lamanan) married (2nd) Bart Lachapelle. No children

On January 1, 1945 Helen Eunice (Crichfield) Gable married (2nd)
Myles Sprague. 2 children

    1. Myles Lamarr Sprague: B. Aug. 19, 1945. He married
    (2.18-1967) Nancy Miles.   2 children

      a.Shelley Sprague: B. March 6, 1968

      b.Steven Sprague: B. Feb. 11, 1971

    2. John Howard Sprague: B. May 17, 1950 (A single man)

****

B. Vida Gertrude Davis: (1891-   )

Vida, the daughter of Mary Marcia (Tallyn) and Daniel Davis, was born in Benson (Woodford Co.,Ill.), October 31,1891. She is a graduate of Benson High School and Shurtleff College (1908) of Alton, Illinois. The latter part of 1908 was spent as a clerk with the Chemical Warfare Service of the War Dept., Washington, D.C. She has her Masters in Psychology from Purdue University (1940). She worked for the State of Indiana for 20 years. As a psychologist she worked in various clinical settings. During this interval she was awarded a fellowship to the Institute of Rehabilitation (New York). She is a member of the American Psychological Association (APA).

On March 15, 1918, Vida married Victor Harvey Davison. They were married at the home of George Potter, Pres. of Shurtleff College. Victor, the son of Paul Harvey and Bertha (Trullender) Davison, was born in Benson (Woodford Co.,Ill.), February 26, 1896. Victor's father, P.H. Davison, came to Woodford County from New York in 1854. He was the first teacher of Clayton Township of Woodford County.

Victor H. Davison interrupted two yrs. of study at the University of Illinois to enlist (Jan. 1918) in the US Air Corps. A mechanic, Victor spent a brief time overseas (England) returning to the U.S. in the fall of 1918. The next ten years were spent in farming in the Bloomington area. From about 1935 until his retirement in 1957 Victor was with the Veterans Administration. During this 22 year interval the family resided in several different cities. After retirement Vida and Victor made their home in Long Beach, California.

Victor Harvey Davison died, July 26, 1968 in Long Beach, Calif. He is buried in the Davison Cemetery, Minonk (Woodford Co.),Illinois. Vida G. (Davis) Davison continues to make her home at Long Beach. Two children were born to the marriage. Both were born in Bloomington, Ill.

1. Morgan Davison: Morgan was born December 23, 1923. He is 1941 graduate of West Lafayette High School and the US Naval Academy (1945). Commander Davison was with the US Navy 25 years prior to retiring in 1970. His many varied responsibilities included: Hurricane Hunter, which involved locating and plotting hurricanes by plane. He is presently an Air Stat Site manager in Nigeria and Meteorologist for TCOM ,Westinghouse.

In Piscagoula, (Miss.) Morgan married (Sept. 26,1948) Laura Anne Anderson. She is the daughter of J.B. and Minnie Anderson. Laura was born, June 6, 1923. Laura was first married to a Mr. Coleman. Judith Anne Coleman was born of this marriage. She was subsequently (1960) adopted into the family of Morgan and Laura.

A. <u>Michael Lee Davison</u>: Michael was born in Portsmouth, Virginia, July 26, 1949.

B. <u>Paul Harvey Davison</u>: Paul was born, January 5, 1952 in Oakland, California. His death occurred October 7, 1961 at age 9.

C. <u>Carol Jane Davison</u>: Carol was born in Jacksonville, Florida, March 19, 1960. She died, May 17, 1964 at age 4.

D. <u>Nancy Laurie Davison</u>: Nancy was born, January 19, 1962 in Jacksonville, Florida.

E. <u>Judith Anne (Coleman) Davison</u>: Judith was born, March 15, 1945 and adopted in 1960. On May 14,1966, at Point Magu, California, Judith married Stephen Grossman. Steve holds the rank of Lt. Commander, U.S. Navy. In August of 1972 they adopted:

      1. <u>Daniel Grossman</u>: B. August 5, 1972

2. <u>Harvey Davison</u>: Harvey, a single man, was born January 25, 1927. He is a graduate of Vincennes High School (Indiana) and De Paul University (Green Castle,Ind.). He worked some ten years in Indianapolis .....partly for the State of Indiana and as a TV announcer. Since 1958 he has been with the Los Angeles County Dept. of Social Services as a supervisor. Harvey is an avid stamp collector.

****

IV. <u>CHARLES ANTHONY TALLYN</u>:(1856-1927)

    Charles, the son of Anthony and Susanna (Lee) Tallyn, was born, August 11, 1856, Peoria County, Illinois. Shortly after, in 1857, the family removed to a farm near Benson of Woodford County, Illinois.

    The <u>1860 U.S. Census</u> for Woodford County lists Charles (age 3) under the household of his father. He appears on the 1870 and 1880 census years as: Charles (age 13) and Charles (age 23),respectively. The <u>1900 US Census</u> for Woodford County lists Charles (age 43), a single man, along with his mother, Susanna (age 76:widow). Hardware Merchant is given as his occupation.

    Charles made his home in Benson where he owned and operated a hardware store. An advertisement in the February 18, 1918 edition of <u>The Benson Bee</u> reads as follows:

CHAS.   TALLYN
General   Hardware   And Repairing
I wish to thank the many friends for their continued patronage and
help, and sincerely trust that you are benefited by our dealing
Chas. Tallyn   Benson, Ill.

37

Charles Anthony Tallyn, a single man, died, March 1, 1927 at age 70. He is buried in Woodford Co.,Illinois.

****

V. CAROLINE SUSANNA TALLYN: (1858-1941):

Caroline or "Carrie", as she was affectionately known, was born, August 28, 1858 in Clayton Township of Woodford County, Illinois. About a year prior to her birth her parents, Anthony and Susanna (Lee) Tallyn, left Peoria County to settle on a farm near the town of Benson.

The great storm of May 13, 1858 destroyed the Tallyn home. A temporary shelter was built to house the family during rebuilding.Carrie was born in this " stable like" structure.

Carrie appears, incorrectly, as <u>Catherine</u> on both the 1860 and 1870 US Census years for Woodford County. The <u>1880 US Census</u> shows her as Carrie age 21. In 1881 she attended a ten week sesson at Valparaiso University.

On February 17, 1892, at age 33, Carrie married Alfred Eugene Forney. Alfred, the son of Adolphus William and Mary Ann (Diehl) Forney, was born in Woodford County, Illinois, March 24, 1863. Shortly after their marriage Carrie and Alfred set up housekeeping on 80 acres owned by Alfred's uncle, Jessie Young Forney. They lived on the farm for the next nine years. Their sons, Emory O. and Roy C. Forney were born there. In February of 1900 Alfred purchased about 160 acres located in the N.W. part of Section 7 of Clayton Township of Woodford County. The family moved in March 1, 1900.

Alfred and Carrie retired from farming in December of 1916. They rented out the farm and moved to Benson.where they lived out their lives. Caroline (Carrie) Susanna (Tallyn) Forney died, November 16, 1941 at age 83. Alfred Eugene Forney died, October 11, 1944 at age 81. Both are buried in Clayton Township Cemetery, Woodford Co., Illinois. Two children were born to the marriage.

1. Emory Owen Forney: 1893-   )

Emory was born, July 11, 1893 in Woodford County. He obtained his elementary and secondary education in the County. He studied piano at Valparaiso University. His studies were interrupted when he enlisted in the US Navy during World War I. He was selected to attend the Navy School of Music at the Great Lakes Naval Training Station. As a trombone player, he played many concerts under the direction of Lt. John Phillip Sousa.......The March King.

On February 12, 1920, Emory married, Ethel Myra Ehringer. She was born, October 5, 1896. Emory and Ethel make their home at Minonk, Illinois, on a portion of the farm once owned by his parents. Emory, retired, has long been interested in family genealogy and is a major contributor to this document. Four children were born to the marriage.

A. Marjorie Elaine Forney: Marjoie was born, November 3, 1923. On March 5, 1950 she married Vernon Dale Pelz (b. Feb. 2, 1918). Marjorie Elaine (Forney) Pelz died, June 24, 1972 at age 48. Vernon's second wife, Marion Elmyra Koch was previously married. She and her 1st. husband had three adopted sons.

Four children were born to Marjorie and Vernon Pelz.

1. Vernon Dale Pelz: Vernon was born, February 9, 1952. He is a 1970 graduate from Minonk-Dana-Rutland High School.(honor student). He has a Bachelor of Science Degree in Agricultural Economics from the U. of Illinois at Urbana (1977). He has a Pilot Certificate and is presently farming near Hillview, Ill.
   On January 9, 1977, Vernon married Carla Haug (b. Jan.28, 1956.).

2. David Randall Pelz: David was born, August 6, 1954. He is a 1972 graduate of Minonk-Dana-Rutland High School. He attended Central Illinois College in East Peoria. He has an Associate Degree in Agricultural Mechanics (1974). Dave is currently farming near Minonk, Illinois. On August 21, 1976, he married Elizabeth (Beth) Clark, born, August 1, 1956.

3. Leigh Annette Pelz: Leigh was born, February 8, 1956. She is a 1974 graduate of Minonk—Dana-Rutland High School.She has a Bachelor of Science Degree in Biology from Bradley University (1978). She subsequently graduated from Medical Technology School at St. Francis Hospital (1979).

4. Lori Suzanne Pelz: Lori was born, September 28, 1958. She graduated from Minonk-Dana-Rutland High School in 1975. She has a Bachelor of Science Degree in Animal Science from Iowa State University at Ames (1979).

B. Lowell Eugene Forney: Lowell was born, January 6, 1926. He is a 1943 graduate of Minonk High School. He served in the US Navy during WW II. His tour of duty included service on the USS Sumter. He saw duty in Siapan, Peleliu and the invasion of Leyte, Luzon and Okinawa. He held the rank of radioman.
   On August 10,1946, Lowell married Lisa Ritschel. She was born December 21,1925. Lowell is engaged in farming near Minonk. He is a member of:American Legion, Farm Bureau Board for Clayton Township and the Baptist Church of Minonk. Six children were born to the marriage.

   1.Claudia Jean Forney: Claudia was born,June 29,1947 in Streator, Illinois. She is a 1969 graduate of Eastern Illinois University (B.S. in Education) and Western Ill. University (M.A. in Music Education: 1979). She is a member of Kappa Delta (sorority) and Sigma Alpha Iota, professional fraternity and Phi Kappa Phi honor society. She is director of the La Harpe Community Chorus. On August 27, 1967, Claudia married James Wendle McCain. James is the Instrumental Music Director for the LaHarpe Schools. 2 children.

      a. James Kristopher McCain: B. Sept 5, 1973.

      b. Chad Owen McCain: B. July 15, 1975

   2. Evan Dale Forney: B. Oct. 17, 1949
                           D..Oct. 17, 1949

3. Sandra Lee Forney: Sandra was born, September 30, 1951,
Streator, Illinois.   She graduated   as a Registered Nurse
from Moline Public Hospital in 1972. She   has an A.A. Degree
from Illinois Central College and a B.S. Degree from Western
Illinois University (1978).Sandra   is working   in obstetrics
at University Hospital in Iowa City. She is a member of the
Baptist Church.

4. Lyle Eugene Forney: Lyle was born, December 13, 1954, at
Streator, Ill. A National Honor Society   student in high
school   he   recieved   a B.A. Degree in Music Education from
Eastern Illinois   University in 1977. He is a member of Phi
Mu Aplha   music fraternity. He presently makes his home in
Flora, Illinois   where he works for Smith Oil Co. He is a
member of the Baptist Church.

5. Kyle David Forney: Kyle was born, October 12, 1962 at
Streator, Ill.   Kyle is attending Minonk-Dana-Rutland
High   School.   His interests include: cross-country track ,
band, chorus, Future Farmers of America, 4H and membership
in the Baptist Church.

6. Susan Kay Forney: Susan   was born in Streator, Illinois,
February 20, 1964.   She is a student at Minonk-Dana-Rutland
High School in Minonk.   Her   activities and interests include   band, chorus,A.F.S., Foriegn Language Club, 4H   and
pianist   for the Minonk First Baptist Church.

C. Melvin Lee Forney: Melvin   was born, January 18, 1931.   He is a
1948   graduate of Minonk High School. He attended Bradley University (2½ yrs). He was in the US Navy (1951-55). He   went
through   pipefitters school at Norfolk, Virginia. His tour of
duty included assignment   aboard the U.S.S. Rehoboth, a survey
ship, which   called   on ports in England, Germany, Scotland,
Ireland, Norway, Denmark, Portugal and others. His medals include:
Good Conduct, National Defense and the European Occupation Medal.
    On April 30, 1953, Melvin married Doris Therese Elbert. Doris
was born, March 10, 1932.   Six children were born to the marriage.

    1. Steven Lee Forney: Steve was born, November 18, 1955.   He
    is a 1973 graduate of Metamora High School and a 2 year
    Member of the National Honor Society. He has a B.S. Degree
    in Mechanical Engineering from the University of Illinois
    at Urbana (1978). He is currently a design engineer at the
    Mossville Plant   of Caterpillar at Mossville, Ill. On Nov.
    29,1976, Steve married Sandra Spangler (b. Oct. 3, 1956).
    They make their home   in Washburn, Ill.   2 children

        a. Lori Ann Forney: B. April 19,1977

        b. Thomas Lee Forney: B. Dec.   20,1978

40

2. Unnamed Infant (female): B. June 13,1957
                                    D. June 13,1957

3. Therese Rose Forney: Therese was born, November 13, 1958. She is a 1976 graduate of Metamora High School and a two year member of the National Honor Society. She has an A.A. Degree in Applied Science from Illinois Central College (1978). She presently works as a Medical Secretary. On April 20, 1979, she married Bruce Allen Smith (b. 11-26-1956). They make their home in El Paso, Illinois. Bruce works for the Shell Chemical Plant.

4. Kevin Joseph Forney: Kevin was born, March 23, 1961. He is a 1979 graduate of Metamora High School and a two year member of the National Honor Society. He served as a Student Council member during is Junior and Senior years and President the Senior year. He was one of three captains of the football team. He plans to pursue a degree in Mechanical Engineering at the U. of Illinois at Urbana...the Fall of 1979.

5. Annette Marie Forney: B. May 20, 1963 Annette is presently attending Metamora High School.

6. Constance Joan Forney: B. September 15, 1965. Connie attends Metamora High School.

4. Eldon Delong Forney: Eldon, the son of Emory and Ethel Forney, was born, November 23, 1934. He obtained his education in the public schools of Minonk, Illinois. He graduated from Minonk-Dana-Rutland High in 1953. On January 16, 1954 he married Joyce Koch. In June of 1953 Eldon moved to Pontiac, Illinois. Eldon worked first on a farm and later as a auto mechanic, starting his own business in 1967. He is presently the Pressroom Superintendent for Johnson Press, Inc. Eldon and Joyce were divorced in 1968.   2 children

    A. Pamela Sue Forney: Pamela was born, January 8, 1955. She is a graduate of Pontiac School System. In Pontiac, she married,September 6, 1975, Tom Harris. Tom is an iron worker. Pam is a secretary , in charge of the Insurance Dept. of Pontiac Saving and Loan.

    B. Paul Owen Forney: Paul was born, January 20, 1959. He is a graduate of the schools of Pontiac, Ill. He is presently a Industrial Technology major at Illinois State University at Normal.....with a 1981 graduation date.

****

Emory and Ethel Forney note they are the progenitors of 4 children, 16 grandchildren of which 4 are great grandchildren.

****

The author is indebted to Emory O. Forney who made his notes ,for the family,available to the author for use in this document.

2. <u>Roy Cranston Forney</u>: (1898   )

     Roy, the son of Alfred E. and Caroline S. (Tallyn) Forney, was born near Benson (Woodford Co.),Illinois, July 18. 1898. He was educated in the schools of the county. Roy retired from farming in 1967. He has demonstrated a long interest in community affairs with a special interest in education and agriculture.
      On February 17, 1921 near Washburn (Woodford Co.), Illinois, Roy married Harriet Pearl Robbins (b. August 9, 1900). Over a period of years they owned and leased several farms in Woodford, Marshall and Bureau counties of Illinois. In 1957 they moved to a recently purchased farm near Varna (Marshall Co.)Illinois where they presently make their home. Six children were born to the marriage.

     A. <u>Ellen Elizabeth Forney</u>: Beth, as she is known, was born October 2, 1923. She is a 1945 college graduate (Home Economics). At the University of Illinois she met Charles Sager Finley (b. June 16, 1922). They were married June 16, 1946 at the home of Beth's parents near Whitefield (Bureau Co.),Illinois. They now make their home at Rockford, Illinois. 6 Children

     1. <u>Carolyn Ruth Finley</u>: Carol was born October 23,1948. On Sept. 7, 1969 at Rockford (Winnebago Co.),Illinois she married Cecil Thomas Highfil (b. March 1, 1945). They make their home near Marion, Kentucky. 2 Children

       a. <u>Cecil Brent Highfil</u>: B. February 26, 1972

       b. <u>Carolyn Jill Highfil</u>: B. July 16, 1974

     2. <u>Stephen Roy Finley</u>: Steven was born August 9, 1951. He is a student at North Texas State University (Denton, Texas).

     3. <u>Jeannette Marlene Finley</u>: She was born September 22,1955. In Rockford, Illinois Jeannette married (April 16, 1977) James William Mays (b. Sept. 20, 1947). Both work for J.L. Clark Co. and they make their home in Rockford, Illinois.

     4.<u>Diane Elizabeth Finley</u>: Diane was born Sept. 12, 1957. She is a Marketing Major in her final year at Western Illinois U. (Macomb, Ill.).

     5.<u>David Reece Finley</u>: David was born August 26, 1961. He presently works for Customized Services of Rockford, Illinois.

     6.<u>Paul Robbins Finley</u>: Paul was born June 16, 1964. He is a student at Thomas Jefferson H.S., Rockford, Illinois.

****

     B. <u>John Richard Forney</u>: John was born August 13, 1925. On February 22, 1948 at Henry (Marshall Co.), Illinois, Richard married Bernice Edna Gibbs (b. Spetember 15, 1927). They first made their home in Saratoga Twp. and subsequently near McNabb, Illinois where in

1960 they purchased their present farm-home they call Melody Lane.

Richard, a farmer-agriculturist, is active in the McNabb Methodist Church, The Magnolia Grange and Mohammed Temple Shrine Band (trumpet) of Peoria, Illinois.   4 Children

1. Nancy Jeanne Forney: Nancy was born January 3, 1951. She is a 1972 graduate of Illinois State University (Normal, Ill.). At Magnolia (Putman Co.),Illinois Nancy married (Feb. 3, 1973) Randall Walter Keller (b. Sept. 13,1950). Both are teachers and work their farm near McNabb, Illinois.

2. Larry Richard Forney: Larry was born June 29, 1952. He is with J.&L. Steel Mill of Mennepin, Illinois. He has his own band and plays the drums.

3. Carol Bernice Forney: Carol was born April 13,1959. She is a junior and Home Ec.major at Western Illinois University, Macomb, Ill.

4. Kathryn Anne Forney: Kathy was born April 30, 1963. She is a Junior at Putman County High School.

*****

C. Ruth Aileen Forney: Ruth was born December 11, 1927. She is a 1948 graduate(R.N.) of St.Frances Hospital and School of Nursing, Peoria, Illinois. On December 5, 1948 Ruth married Jack Wallace Rogers. He was born, July 20, 1925. (Now Divorced) They first made their home in Pekin, Illinois. In 1959 the family moved to Colorado and later Las Vegas, Nevada where Ruth is with Sunrise Hospital.   4 children

1. John Wallace Rogers: John was born August 16,1949. He is employed and lives in Las Vegas, Nevada.

2. Ann Marie Rogers: Ann was born October 14,1950.In Las Vegas, Nevada Ann married (May 28, 1972) John Hartley Perry (b. Aug. 4, 1951). They make their home in Warren, Pennsylvania. 2 Children

a. Michael John Perry: B. May 19, 1973

b. Victoria Lynde Perry: B. July 29, 1974

3. Elizabeth Jeanne Rogers: Elizabeth was born January 23, 1952. In Loveland (Larimer Co.),Colorado, Beth married (Dec. 1, 1973) John Elmer Woelfle, III. He was born June 7, 1949. They make their home in Live Creek, Colorado.   1 Child

a. Mathew Jason Woelfle: B. November 29,1974

4. James Cranston Rogers: Jim was born August 16, 1953.He works and makes his home in Las Vegas, Nevada.

****

* Ruth Aileen Forney was married near Whitefield (Bureau Co.), Illinois.

Mrs. Alfred E. Forney
(Caroline Susanna Tallyn)

1858-1941

Daughter of Anthony and
Susanna (Lee) Tallyn

Photos Courtesy of:

    Mrs. John Mudry
(Franklin Lakes, N.J.)

Countryside near
Brayford of North
Devon England

Anthony Tallyn was
baptized in the
Church at Brayford

December 25, 1843

D. Robert Cranston Forney: Robert was born April 10,1932. He
served in the U.S. Army. A portion of his tour of duty was at Ft.
Collins, Colorado. In Chicago (Cook Co.), Illinois Robert married
(Dec. 27,1935) Dorothy Ann Drozd (b. July 26,1934). Robert is a
1961 graduate of the University of Illinois College of Dentistry.
In Plano, Texas Dr. Robert Forney designed and built the dental complex where he has his practice.   1 Child

    1. Lynette Joy Forney: Lynette was born Sept. 4, 1956. She is
a graduate of Texas Tech University (Lubbock, Texas). She attended
(1 yr.) the International School of Advertising (Paris) and is presently with Bloom Advertising Agency of Dallas, Texas.

****

    E. Harriet Jeanne Forney: Harriet was born near Varna, Illinois
April 25, 1935. She attended schools in Varna and Henry, Ill. She is
a graduate of the U..of Illinois College of Nursing and the Methodist
Hospital School of Nursing.
   On August 8, 1959 at the Methodist Church of Varna(Marshall Co.),
Illinois Harriet married John Paul Mudry. He is the son of Paul and
Elizabeth (Saldon) Mudry. He was born August 9, 1932 Cliffside Park,
New Jersey. John Paul Mudry, M.D., is a graduate of the University of
Chicago College of Medicine. He did a residency in Internal Medicine.
Dr. Mudry served in the U.S. Navy. At various times the family has
made its home in Chicago, Washington, D.C. and New Jersey. The family
presently resides in Franklin Lakes, New Jersey..Dr. Mudry has his
practice in nearby Ridgewood, N.J.
   Harriet(Forney) Mudry is active in community, school and church
related groups and activies. She is a member of the American Guild
of Organists. The family is active in the Grace Methodist Church.
4 Children

    1. Carolyn Jeanne Mudry: Carolyn was born in Washington,D.C.
April 10, 1962. She attended schools in Wyckoff and Franklin Lakes,
N.J. Her plans include a college major in art. Carolyn teaches Sun-
day School at the Grace Methodist Church.

    2. Patricia Pearl Mudry: Patricia was born December 8, 1964
in Ridgeway (Bergen Co.),New Jersey. She is active in youth activities,
soccer and plays violin in the school orchestra.She attended schools
in Wyckoff and Franklin Lakes, N.J. She is a member of the Grace
Methodist Church.

    3. Kathryn Elizabeth Mudry: Kathryn was born in Ridgeway,
November 4, 1966. She attends school in Franklin Lakes (N.J.) and is
a cheerleader. She attends Grace Methodist Church and is active in
Youth Fellowship. Her interests include drawing and oil painting.

    4. John Robert Mudry: John was born December 6, 1968 in
Ridgeway, N.J. He attends school in Franklin Lakes. He plays trumpet
in the school band and is in Junior Football League. He attends the
Grace Methodist Church Sunday School.

****

F. Roger Franklin Forney: Roger, the son of Roy and Harriet (Robbins) Forney, was born December 7, 1938. On May 31, 1956, in McNabb (Putnam Co.),Illinois, Roger married Donna M. Orasser. She was born Sept. 20, 1938. Roger, a farmer, also works for Goodrich Checmical, Henry, Illinois and is active in school and community affairs .   4 children.

     1. Deborah Susan Forney: Deborah was born August 17, 1957. On August 13,1977 in Princeton (Bureau Co.), Illinois, she married Rodney Warren Pinter (b. May 21,1955). Rodney is a graduate of Illinois Valley Community College and is with Colonial Trust and Savings Bank of Peru, Illinois.

     2. Wendy Lee Forney: Wendy was born June 30, 1959. She is a Junior and Business Major at Western Illinois University, Macomb, Illinois.

     3. Todd Alan Forney: Todd was born August 3, 1961.He is a pre-dentistry student at Illinois Valley Community College.

     4. Kristine Jo Forney: Kristy was born October 12, 1968. She is a student at John Sweney Grade School.

****

The author is indebted to Elizabeth "Beth" (Forney) Finley of Rockford, Illinois and Emory O. Forney of Minonk, Illinois who made their records concerning the family and descendants of Roy and Harriet (Robbins) Forney available for use in this document.

Mrs. John Mudry (Harriet J. Forney) of Franklin Lakes, New Jersey, is the major contributor of information to that segment pertaining to the family of Dr. and Mrs. John Mudry.

****

Of Genealogical Interest

Three set of twins have been born to the descendants of William R. Tallyn of Stoke Rivers of Devon, England. They include:

     1. Joseph and Judson Piche B. November 17, 1922. They are the children of Fern (Pickard) and Thomas Piche and the great grandsons of Anthony and Susanna (Lee) Tallyn

     2. Terry Ann and Thomas Henry Tallyn B..February 23, 1957. They are the children of George Bernard and Helen (Burgess)Tallyn and great grandchildren of Joseph and Sarah (Daniel) Tallyn.

     3. Karla and Marla Wolf B. October 30, 1972. They are the children of Arlene (Tallyn) and Donald Wolf and the great grand-daughters of Joseph and Sarah A. (Daniel) Tallyn.

****

46

VI. JOHN FRANKLIN TALLYN: (1861-1863)

John, the son of Anthony and Susanna (Lee) Tallyn, was born in Woodford County, Illinois, March 20, 1861. On Monday, February 16, 1863 he took ill. John Franklin Tallyn died, Wednesday, February 18, 1863 one month prior to his 2nd birthday.

The events surrounding his illness and death are contained in a letter made available to the author by Emory O. Forney of Minonk, Illinois. The letter is dated February 20, 1863. It is from Anthony and Susanna Tallyn to Thomas R. and Elizabeth (Fry) Tallyn of Peoria County. Excerpts of this letter are presented below.

" Dear Brother and Sister...

It is with sorrow of heart that I write this line or two, our dear dear little Frankie died Wednesday morning about nine o'clock or some after. Yesterday we followed his remains to his last resting place till the ressurection morn. It as so sudden and unexpected by me that I can hardly fancy he is really gone from us. We was at Robert Shambrooks a few hours on Sunday, tooked him and Carrie along he enjoyed himself fine in play. Monday he seemed rather unwell but was around all day. Monday night he had some fevor, Tuesday he was pretty sick but I thot with a little medicine he would get along as many children around had that has been quiet complaining. I went to Minonk did not get back again till night there he was pretty sick through the night did not have so much fever but was very distressed to get his breth. Wednesday morning we sent for the doctor but he had left the day before. When the boy came back from Minonk we sent him right out for another doctor. He had only been gone about a half hour when he   slept away without a struggle......
We remain your Sister and Brother........ "

(signed)   S & A Tallyn

****

John Franklin Tallyn was first buried in the Old Clayton Cemetery. In the Summer of 1912 his remains were moved to the New Clayton Cemetery . The land,consisting of 5 acres, was formerly owned by Anthony and Susanna (Lee) Tallyn.

****

---

1   This section was based on the notes, records and recollections of Emory O. Forney of Minonk, Illinois. The author is indebted to Mr. Forney for making them available for use in this document.

VII.   FREDERICK NEWTON ROWE TALLYN:(1864-1942)

Frederick, the son of Anthony and Susanna (Lee) Tallyn, was born, January 30, 1864 in Clayton Township of Woodford County, Illinois. He appears on the 1870 US Census for the County under the household of his recently widowed mother, Susanna as: Freddy age 6. In 1880 he is listed as: Frederick: age 16.

Frederick attended Knox College of Galesburg, Ill. He was president of the First National Bank of Benson. Various Benson editions of the Benson Bee refer to him as F.N. Tallyn and that is how his name appeared on official bank documents. He was active in the Baptist Church of Benson and served on the board as a deacon.

On September 24, 1890, Frederick married (1st) Emilie Lee Fry. She was the daughter of John and Susan (Lee) Fry. Emilie was born, May of 1862. (Another source has her born : March 26, 1866) Emilie was born in Stoke Rivers of Devon England. The Fry family came to the US in 1866. (See Fry Family in Appendix)

The family made their home in Benson. The 1900 US Census for Woodford County lists the family as follows:

TALLYN, Fred	age 36	B. Jan. 1864	10yrs.Married	Chashier	B. Ill.
(w) Emilie	38	May. 1862	" " To US in 1866		England
(d) Alpha	7	May 1893			Ill.
(s) Gordon	4	Apr. 1896			Ill.
(d) Beth	1	May. 1899			Ill.
John Fry	63	Nov. 1837	Druggist: To US in 1866		England
(Father-in-law to Fred Tallyn)					

****

Emilie Lee (Fry) Tallyn died, January 20,1915 at age 49. She is buried at Benson. On July 9, 1923, Frederick married (2nd) Emmaline Similie who had been previously married to a Mr. Eberlein. Emmaline died, August 5, 1939. No children were born to this marriage. Frederick continued to make his home in Benson. Two days prior to his death he suffered a stroke which impaired his orientation capacities. On the evening of February 17, 1942 he was struck and killed by a train while walking the track near Benson (Minonk News-Dispatch: Feb. 19,1942). Frederick Newton Rowe Tallyn is buried at Benson, Woodford Co.,Illinois. 3 children

1. ALPHA MAY TALLYN:(1893-1978)

Alpha was born, May 23, 1893 at Benson. In Benson she married, Sept., 9, 1916, Bruce Henry Kindig. He was born in Woodford County, July 9, 1891. Bruce was one of four children born to John Martin and Ella Frances (Lantz) Kindig (See Kindig Family in Appendix) The Benson Bee newpaper indicates B.H. Kindig was a Notary Public of Woodford Co. (1918).

Bruce H. Kindig died, August 8, 1976. Alpha May (Tallyn) Kindig died, March 25, 1978. Both are buried at Godfrey (Madison Co.), Illinois. 3 children

A. Gwendolyn Ruth Kindig: Gwendolyn was born in Benson, June 17, 1917. On January 17, 1941 she married Milan L. Warford who was born, Sept. 27, 1915. Six children were born to the marriage.

1. Susan Beth Warford: B. March 6, 1942

2. David Allen Warford:David was born, January 4, 1945. He
   married, June 10, 1967, Susan Elizabeth Cooke. 2 children

    a. Thomas Murray Warford: B. April 26, 1968

    b. Tina Resanne Warford: B. Sept. 28, 1970

3.Diane Elizabeth Warford: Diane was born, November 21,1947.
   On Sept. 23, 1972 she married Dr. R. Brian Ullman. 1 child

    a.Elizabeth VanWay Ullman: B. December 30, 1976 at
   Ridgewood, New Jersey.

4. Thomas Richard Warford: B. December 11, 1948

5. James Richard Warford: B. September 15, 1952

6. Robert Louis Warford: B. September 13, 1954
                    ****
B. Jack Tallyn Kindig: Jack   was born, August 17, 1922/23 (?)
in Peoria , Illinois. On March 22, 1947 , in Centralia, Illinois,
he married, Barbara Storer.* 3 children

1. Kerry Douglas Kindig: B. Dec. 5, 1950 Alton, Illinois

2. Kathy Jo Kindig: B. Apr. 22,1959 St. Louis, Mo.

3. Stephen John Kindig: B.July 21,1962 Naples, Florida

                    ****
C. Malcom Lee Kindig: Malcom was born in Peoria,Illinois, July 21,
1928. In Alton (Madison Co.),Illinois, he married (Sept. 5, 1953),
Viola Annamae Neuhaus. Viola, the daughter of Raymond Adolphus and
Verna Viola (Heyen) Neuhaus, was born, May 13, 1932 in Litchfield,
Illinois.   3 children

1. Mathew Lee Kindig: B. May 25, 1959 Chicago, Illinois

2. Mark William Kindig:B. June 20,1960 Alton, Illinois

3. Stacey Ann Kindig: B. June 11, 1964 St. Louis, Missouri
                    ****

2. GORDON CLEMENT TALLYN: (1896-1974)

     Gordon, the son of Frederick and Emilie (Fry) Tallyn, was born
in Benson, April 5, 1896. He obtained his elementary and secondary
education in the public schools of Woodford County, Illinois. He
attended Shurtleff College at Alton, Illinois. His studies were interrupted by the onset of WW I. At Camp Pike, Little Rock, Arkansas,
he was trained as an engineer. His unit,CO E of the 312th Engineers
(US Army Corp.),served in France. While in Europe Gordon visited

----

* Barbara was born, August 13,1926.

                              49

Scotland and England. In Devon, England he stayed overnight at Lower Davis of Stoke Rivers, where his grandmother, Susanna (Lee) Tallyn was born.

Gordon married, May 31, 1918, Edith Blanche Milford. They were married in Little Rock, Arkansas just three months before he set sail for Europe. Edith, the daughter of Richard James and Mary (Ross) Milford, was born in Tribune, Kansas, March 16, 1896. Edith also attended Shurtleff College.

After the war Gordon and Edith made their home in Benson, Illinois. He was head cashier in the First State Bank of Benson until the crash of 1929. He subsequently worked for Shell Oil of Roxanna, Illinois. The last forty years of his life was spent in Alton, Illinois. He was with the Alton State Hospital as a stationary engineer in the power plant. Gordon was an active member of the Baptist Church of Alton and served on the church board as financial secretary, treasurer and deacon.

Gordon Clement Tallyn, former mayor of Benson, suffered a fatal heart attack, April 25, 1974. His death occurred in Potomac (Vermilion Co.), Illinois at age 78. He is buried in Valhalla Memorial Park Cemetery, Godfrey (Madison Co.), Illinois. He was preceded in death by his wife, Edith Blanche (Milford)Tallyn. Edith died in Winslow, Arizona, May 28, 1971. On June 1, 1971 she was buried at Godfrey (Madison Co.), Illinois. Four children were born to the marriage.

A. Nevalee Tallyn: Nevalee was born, July 3, 1920 in Peoria County, Illinois. She is a graduate of Shurtleff College. She has a Masters Degree from the U. of Illinois at Urbana. She taught at the elementary level prior to marriage. She is a life-long member of the Baptist Chruch. On June 7, 1948 at Champaign, Illinois, she married Dr. John H. Johnson. John, the son of Oscar C. and Maude (Harpster) Johnson, was born, May 21,1921, Perrysburg, Ohio. John has a Bachelor Degree from the U. of Toledo and Doctorate from U. of Illinois (Champaign-Urbana).
Dr. John Johnson is a bio-medical researcher with Monsanto of St. Louis, Missouri. 4 children

1. Marcia Lee Johnson: Marcia was born, May 22, 1950, Harvey (Cook Co.),Illinois. She grew up in Dayton, Ohio and Kirkwood, Missouri. She has a Bachelors Degree from So. Missouri State University (Cape Girardeau, Mo.) She taught in the elementary schools of St. Louis, Mo. and Mobile, Alabama.
On December 29, 1973 at Richmond Heights (St. Louis) Marcia married Steven Carter Dawson. Steven, the son of William Roy Dawson (Jr) and Carol McCullum, was born, Oct. 6, 1950. Steve has a Bachelors Degree (Marine Biology) from C.W. Post Div. of Long Island University (N.Y.). He is working on a Doctorate at U. of Alabama at Mobile.

2. Cynthia Jane Johnson: Cynthia was born, April 29, 1952, Dayton (Montgomery Co.),Ohio. She has a Bachelors Degree (Speech Pathology) for the U. of Iowa (Iowa City).She has her Docorate (Communication Disorders) from the U. of Minnesota. She is presently Asst. Prof. at Northwestern University (Evanston, Ill.). In Iowa City, Iowa, she married (May 29,1974) Bruce Edward Schiel. Bruce was born, May 13,1952 in Dubuque, Iowa. He is the son of John Paul

and Virginia (McPoland) Schiel. Bruce attended the U. of
Iowa and the U. of Minnesota at St. Paul. He is a computer
operator at Northwestern University at Evanston. Cynthia re-
tained her maiden name after marriage.

3. Karen Sue Johnson: Karen was born, April 22, 1955, Dayton
(Montgomery Co.),Ohio. Her early years were spent in Dayton,
Ohio and Kirkwood, Missouri. She has a B.S. Degree in Psychology from the U. of Missouri (at Columbia) and is working
on a Masters at the U. of Minnesota (at St. Paul). She is a
member of Phi Beta Kappa. She works summers as assistant director of a Y Camp.

4. Dennis Tallyn Johnson: Dennis was born in Dayton, Ohio,
March 7, 1959. His youth was spent in Dayton, Ohio and Kirk-
wood, Missouri. He attends the U. of Missouri (at Columbia).
He spent a summer in Sao Paulo, Brazil as a participant in the
Youth For Understanding exchange program.

B. Carol Elaine Tallyn: Carol, was born in Peoria, Illinois, Dec.
25, 1922. She spent her youth in Benson, Roxana and Alton, Illinois.
She is a graduate Registered Nurse (School of Nursing:Alton Memorial
Hospital). In Wright City, Missouri she married, Jan. 22, 1943, Ellis
John Gaston, Jr. He is the son of Ellis Joseph and Freda Marie (Thompson) Gaston. Ellis was born, April 12, 1923, Alton, Illinois. Ellis,
an ordained minster, is a graduate of Moody Bible Institute.
   Carol and Rev. Gaston have worked with the Navajo and Hopi Indians
of Arizona and New Mexico for the past 25 years.They founded and built
the Navajo Baptist Church at Winslow, Arizona. They presently reside
at Jones Ranch Station near Vanderwagen, New Mexico, where they conduct
bible camps for the Indians.   7 children

1. Cheri Ann Gaston: B. May 18, 1944 Kokomo, Indiana. On July
12,1962, Winslow, Arizona, she married Eugene Karleton Kirby.
Eugene was born, July 8, 1938. 2 children

          a. Kris Karleton Kirby: B. Oct. 24,1963 Phoenix, Airz.

          b.Wendy Joell Kirby: B. Nov. 28, 1966 Fullerton, Calif.

2.Jennifer Jill Gaston: B. Feb. 3, 1947 Alton(Madison Co.),Ill.
In Winslow, Arizona she married (Aug. 11,1966) Walter Neil Brake.
Walter was born, August 24, 1946. Four children .(All were born
in Mesa, Arizona).

          a. Lynde Jean Brake: B. Feb. 24, 1970
          b. Elena Marie Brake: B. Jan. 3, 1975
          c. Brian Nathaneil Brake: B. Mar. 24, 1977
          d. Walter Michael Gaston Brake   B. Feb. 23, 1978

3. Elaine Marie Gaston: Elaine was born, August 9, 1948, Alton,
Illinois. In Winslow, Arizona, Elaine, married(Aug. 16,1969),
Fred Ube Reiter. He was born, Nov. 9, 1948. 4 Children

    a. Fred Ellis Reiter: B. Mar. 10,1971   Winslow, Ariz.
    b. Jill Marie Reiter: B. May 17,1972   Munich, Germany
    c. Joanna Salome Reiter: B. Apr. 12,1976   Salem, Oregon
    d. Felissa Lynn Reiter: B. Dec. 30,1977   Carnation,Wash.

4. Ellis Jeffrey Gaston, III: Ellis was born, March 19, 1951,
Chicago (Cook Co.), Illinois.

5. Mathew John Gaston: Mathew was born, Sept. 7, 1952, Chicago,
Illinois.On November 16, 1974 in Jacksonville, Florida, Mathew
married, Deborah Elaine Loyless. Deborah, the daughter of Charles E. and Ann Loyless, was born, July 18,1952. 2 children

    a. Allison Rene Gaston: B. October 25, 1975

    b. Charles Ellis Gaston: B. December 2, 1977

6. Timothy Gordon Gaston: Timothy was born, January 5, 1954
Alton, Illinois. In San Antonio, Texas Tim married (July 4,
1978) Patricia Loreine Norman. She is the daughter of Richard
and Barbara Norman.

7. Joseph Clement Gaston: Joseph was born, June 15, 1957
Winslow, Arizona. Joseph died suddenly, July 2, 1971 at age
14.

The children of Elaine and Rev. Ellis Gaston have attended
college and some have graduated. Two daughters married ministers and
one a teacher. One son is a minister...one works for an architect and
one is in management.

****

C.Milford Gordon Tallyn:

    Milford, the son of Gordon and Edith (Milford) Tallyn, was born
August 17, 1925, Peoria (Peoria Co.),Illinois. He spent his early years
in Benson, Roxana and Alton, Illinois. He served in the US Army, 397th
Infantry Div., in France. He was wounded in action, Nov. 13, 1944. After
being hospitalized for 10 months in France, England and the U.S. he was
discharged. He attended the U. of Kansas(at Lawrence) Army Specialized
Training Program. He attended Rubicam Business College(St. Louis, Mo.),
& Shurtleff College at Alton, Ill. For three years he worked for United
Bank of St Louis. For the past 30 years he has worked (Accounting Super-
visor) for American Investment Co.
    On December 28, 1945, in Alton, Illinois, Milford married, Jean
Marjorie Herzberger. Jean, the daughter of Carl Henry George and Irene
Gertrude (Seddon) Herzberger,was born, December 18, 1925,O'Fallon,
St. Clair County, Illinois. Jean also attended Shurtleff College.
They have made their home in St Louis, Missouri since 1960. Prior to
1960 Milford was a Baptist.After the move to St. Louis he became a
member of the United Church of Christ. He has served on the board as
financial secretary and treasurer.   3 children

1. <u>John Seddon Tallyn</u>: John was born in Alton (Madison Co.), Illinois, February 14, 1948. He spent his youth in Alton and St. Louis, Missouri. He is a 1972 graduate of Purdue University(B.S. Degree:Civil Engineering).He was a member of the Perdue Marching Band and performed in the Rose Parade and Rose Bowl (Pasadena, Cal.) and in Venezuela and Columbia, S.A.

On June 6, 1970 in Lafayette, Indiana, John married, Eva Jane Mankey. Eva, the daugher of Dale Edward and Lorena (Huffman) Mankey, was born, January 30, 1949, Bluffton, Indiana. Jean has a B.S. Degree (Vocational Home Economics Education) from Purdue and a Masters (Early Childhood Educ.) from the U. of Illinois. John works(Chief Estimating Eng.) for the Illinois Central Gulf Railroad. He is a member of the United Church of Christ and is on the board. 2 children

    a. <u>Nicholas Kyle Tallyn</u>: B. Apr. 13, 1975   Urbana, Illinois

    b. <u>Matthew Wade Tallyn</u>: B. Apr. 23, 1978   Harvey, Illinois

2. <u>Kent Lee Tallyn</u>: Kent was born, November 30, 1952, Alton (Madison Co.), Illinois. He grew up in Alton, Illinois and St. Louis, Missouri. where he presently makes his home. Kent has a B.S. Degree (Electrical Engineering) from the U. of Missouri at Rolla (1974).He has completed some of the requirements leading to the Masters. He is employed as an electronics engineer at McDonnell Douglas Astronautics Co., St. Louis, Mo. He is a licensed pilot and owns his own plane. He is a member of the United Church of Christ.

3. <u>Sue Jean Tallyn</u>: Sue lived her early years in Alton, Illinois and St. Louis Missouri, where she now resides. Sue was born, September 7, 1956, at Alton, Illinois. She received an Associate Degree in Child Care and Guidance from S. E. Missouri State University (Cape Girardeau, Mo.) and a B.S. Degree (Elementary Education) from South East Missouri State University (1979). She is a member of the United Church of Christ.

****

D.   <u>Dorothy Theon Tallyn</u>:

      Dorothy, the daughter of Gordon and Edith(Milford) Tallyn, was born, September 8. 1929, Peoria, Illinois. She grew up in Benson and Roxana, Illinois. She completed work on her Bachelors Degree at Greenville College.(Greenville, Ill.)She has completed some graduate studies at U. of Illinois (Champaign-Urbana) and courses at Moody Bible Institute of Chicago. She taught elementary grades in Mowequa, Roxana and Potomac, Illinois.

On December 28, 1959, in Alton (Madison Co.), Illinois, Dorothy married, Len Stuby. Len, the son of Elmer Everett and Elsie Lily (Mulligan) Stuby, was born, May 29, 1932.   Len, a teacher, received his Bachelors from East. Illinois U. (Charleston, Ill.) and Masters   the University of Illinois (Champaign-Urbana). Len was a teacher. He taught high school mathematics in Skokie, Champaign and Armstrong, Illinois.

Len Stuby died, March 3, 1974, Potomac(Vermilion Co.), Ill.
He is buried at Bethalto, Madison Co.,Illinois.   4 children

    1. <u>Kevin Lee Stuby</u>:   B. May 29,1962 Paxton, Illinois

    2. <u>Leigh Ann Stuby</u>:   B. Mar. 25,1964 Paxton, Illinois

    3. <u>Donna Marie Stuby</u>:   B. Jan. 21,1966 Urbana, Illinois

    4. <u>Sue Jean Stuby</u>:   B. Feb. 12,1968 Urbana, Illinois

****

3. <u>BETH JEANETTE TALLYN</u>:

    Beth, the daughter of Frederick Newton and Emilie Lee (Fry)
Tallyn, was born in May of 1899, Benson (Woodford Co.), Illinois.
Beth appears on the <u>1900 US Census of Woodford County</u> under the
household of her father, F.N. Tallyn. She appears as:

        Beth   age 1   Born: May 1899
    Beth Jeanette Tallyn died, March 16, 1901, at age 1 year and 10
months. She is most likely buried in Woodford County, Illinois.

******

ACKNOWLEDGEMENT

    The preparation of this section on the children and descendants of
Frederic Newton and Emilie (Fry) Tallyn was substantially aided by
the efforts , notes and records of:

        <u>Milford G. Tallyn</u> of St. Louis, Missouri

             and

        <u>Emory O. Forney</u>: of   Minonk, Illinois

****

This concludes the   listing of the children and descendants of Anthony
Tallyn (1823-1867) and Susanna (Lee) Tallyn (1823-1912).

IV. MARY TALLYN:[1]

     Mary, the daughter of William R. and Mary Tallyn, was born about 1826 at Birch Farm of the Parish of Stoke Rivers. Mary is enumerated on the 1841 Census for Stoke Rivers under the household of her father, William. She is listed as being age 15.

    In 1849 Mary married Thomas Ridd. The event is recorded in Barnstaple Marriages Vol. X, page 76, 1849. Mary and Thomas made their home at Southcott of Bratton Fleming. The Church of England Christening Records for Bratton Fleming, indicate their first child, William Ridd, was christened, September 26,1849.

    The 1851 Census for Bratton Fleming shows the family at Southcott as follows:

****

Thomas Ridd		age 32	Farmer	50 acres	B. Wales
(w)	Mary	25			Stoke Rivers
(s)	William	1			Bratton Fleming

****

Also listed under the household of Thomas Ridd is: Sarah Larney (servant) Agnes Ridd (servant) William Ridd (servant)William Lewis (servant) John Brooks(servant) and William Muxworthy.

    Ten years later, the 1861 Census for Bratton Fleming lists the family as follows:

Thomas Ridd		age 40	Farmer	150 acres	B. Wales	
(w)	Mary	36			Stoke Rivers	
(s)	William	11			Bratton Fleming	
(s)	John	9			"	"
(d)	Ellen	7			"	"
(d)	Elizabeth	2			"	"

The household also includes:

William Ridd	38	Shepard	Challacombe	
William Kingdom	26	Carder	Bratton Fleming	
John Crallon	12	Carder	"	"
Elizabeth Crallon	20	House Servant	"	"

****

    Mary(Tallyn)Ridd   died around May of 1864 at about age 38. She is most likely buried at Stoke Rivers or Bratton Fleming.

    Around the Fall of 1864 a portion of the family left England to settle in America. They settled in Jo Daviess County, Illinois. At some point between 1864 and the taking of the 1870 census, Thomas remarried.

---

1 Sources for this segment include: 1841,1851 and 1861 census for Stoke Rivers and Bratton Fleming; Church of England christening records for Bratton Fleming, Barnstaple Marriages and the 1900, 1880 and 1870 census(U.S.) for Jo Daviess County, Illinois. The author is also indebted to Emory O. Forney of Minonk, Illinois for making his notes on the Ridd family available for use in this document.

The <u>1870 US Census for West Galena of JoDaviess Co...</u>lists two entries for the family.

(1) West Galena

<u>Ridd, Thomas</u>	age 50	Farmer	B. Wales
(w) Hannah	54		England
(s) Thomas*	12		England

(2) Galena

<u>Ridd, William</u>	age 20	Dry Goods Clerk	England
John	18	" " "	"
(brother to Wm.)			

****

* Thomas (age 12) may or may not be the son of Thomas and Mary (Tallyn) Ridd. His age indicates he was born around 1856. He is not listed along with the family on the <u>1861 Census for Bratton Fleming</u>.

****

Ellen (1854) and Elizabeth Ridd (1859) appear not to have made the trip to America. They may have remained in England with relatives or friends

William and John Ridd first made their home in America with the family of Horatio Henry Chandler of Galena. The Chandlers were also from England. They owned and managed a dry goods store at Galena.

Around 1875 William Ridd married Louisa Fritz. Louisa, the daughter of John and Regula (Blumer) Fritz, was born in East Galena of Jo Daviess County, Ill.   Her siblings included: <u>John</u> (1854) and <u>Mary</u> Fritz (1858). John Fritz (Sr.) came to America in 1846.

John Fritz was a cabinet maker and owner of the J. Fritz Sash, Door and Blind Factory of Galena. William Ridd went to work for his father-in-law. He later became a member of the firm. He was a noted business man of Galena.

The <u>1880 US Census for (Galena) JoDaviess Co.,Ill.</u>, shows the family as follows:

****

<u>Ridd, William</u>	age 30	Clerk in Sash Factory	B. England
(w) Louisa	38	Keeping House	Illinois
(d) Edith	4		"
(s) Willie	3 months		"

****

Residing nearby in West Galena of the County:

<u>Ridd, Thomas</u>	age 62	Farmer	B. Wales
(h) Hannah	68	Keeping House	Warickshire, England
(s) Thomas	24	Farming	Wales

****

****

Ridd, William	b. August 1849	age 50	Married 27yrs.	B.England
(w) Louisa	b. Nov. 1851	48	" " "	B. Illinois
(d) Edith	b. Nov. 1875	24	_____	B. "
(s) William T.	b. Jan. 1880	20	_____	B. "

William indicates his parents were both born in England. He indicates he came to the US 36 years ago in 1864. Louisa notes that her father was born in Germany and her mother, Switzerland.

****

It is difficult to disentangle the many Ridd families of North Devon. This would be necessary to determine the parents of Thomas Ridd, the husband of Mary (Tallyn) Ridd. There are several Ridd families residing in Stoke Rivers, Bratton Fleming and nearby Loxhore.....as early as 1841. Ridd is one of the oldest family surnames found in North Devon. The following data is presented because of its genealogical interest.

1880 US Census East Galena Jo Daviess Co., Illinois:

FRITZ, John	age 57	Sash Factory	B. Wurtenburg (Germany)
(w)Regula	56	Keeping house	B. Switzerland
(s) John	26	Works in Sash Factory	B. Illinois
(d) Mary	22	Clerk in Dry Goods Store	B. Illinois

****

1870 US Census East Galena Jo Daviess Co.,Illinois:

Chandler, H.H.	age 38	Dry Goods Merchant	B. England
(w) Annie	32	Keeping House	B. England
Emma	11	at school	B. Illinois
Frank	8	_____	"
Fannie	6	_____	"
Alice	4	_____	"
Mary	1	_____	"

****

Horatio Henry Chandler was the youngest of nine children. He was born in England, December 4, 1831. He came to the US in 1852. His first wife, Annie Holder, died July 1874. They were married in 1858. Annie was reared in Gloucestershire, England. Horatio married (2nd) Emma Shaw, July 18, 1877. She was born in Lincolnshire, the daughter of Robert and Rebecca Shaw of Swineshead, England. Horatio started the Dry Goods Store at East Galena with his brother-in-law, John G. Baker. John married Fanny J. Chandler, Horatio's sister.

****

THE FAMILY OF JOSEPH AND SARAH A.(DANIEL) TALLYN

Back Row: Left to Right

| Lizzie | Newton | Sarah | Louis | Arthur | Alice | Edwin |
| Eva | Oscar | Irene | Liston | Herbert | Agusta | Maurice |

Front Row: Left to Right

William Henry   Joseph   Sarah   Ella Frances

****

Missing is <u>Newton Elmore Tallyn</u> who died in infancy

V. JOSEPH TALLYN (1829-1902)

Joseph, the son of William R. and Mary Tallyn, was born, April 19, 1829, Stoke Rivers of Devon, England. There is little information concerning his youth and early manhood spent in his native Devon. Joseph (age 12) and his brothers,Anthony and George do not appear , along with the rest of the family, on the 1841 Census for Stoke Rivers. There is reason to believe that something took place around this time (1841) to disrupt the family unit. For example, Mary the wife of William R. Tallyn, is not listed on the 1841 census. William's mother, Charity(widow age 70) appears in her place.

Joseph, Anthony and George may have left (apprenticed out)to learn trades. Emory O. Forney of Minonk, Illinois, recalls seeing his grandfather's (Anthony Tallyn) large pressing irons. Edwin W. Tallyn of Walnut Creek, California, notes Joseph too was a tailor and worked at his trade in his native Devon prior to coming to America. Joseph may have worked as a tailor in Bristol of North Devon just prior to coming to America. If so this might account for an entry in the 1913 Alumuni Record, University of Illinois. In this reference, Louis Tallyn, the youngest child of Joseph Tallyn, indicates his father was born in Bristol, England.

In 1850 Joseph Tallyn left England for America. He first settled in Kickapoo of Peoria County, Illinois. He was very likely met by his brothers Anthony and Thomas who had settled in the county earlier. Joseph, his brothers and others were instrumental in organizing (1851) the Kickapoo Baptist Church.

On March 31, 1855, in Kickapoo, Joseph married Sarah A. Daniel. Sarah, the daugher of George and Emma Daniel, was born, December 18, 1833. Parish records (Church of England) for Contisbury of North Devon indicate Sarah was christened, February 2, 1834. Sarah came to America in 1851 with the family of her cousin Ann Conibear. (See Daniel and Conibear Families in Appendix for additional information).

Joseph and Sarah first made their home in Kickapoo where son, William Henry Tallyn was born. In October of 1856 Joseph purchased 160 acres of undeveloped prairie land in Section 29 of Clayton township of Woodford Co., Illinois. Emory O. Forney (Minonk, Ill.) notes that Joseph and Anthony bought adjoining farms. Each put up a division fence. The two foot space between the two fences they called,"Devil's Lane".

Around 1858 Joseph and the family moved onto the Clayton township farm. Their first home was a log cabin. A home built later, still stands. Many years of effort were required to break, develop and cultivate the prairie and turn it into a productive farm.

Joseph, Anthony and others help establish (1859) the Old Clayton Baptist Church. Members first met in homes for prayer and song singing. A church was built in 1865. It was replaced by the Baptist Church of Benson in 1874.(See Verna (Tallyn) Herbst in Bibliography)

The 1860 US Census , Woodford County, Illinois provides an early record of the family in the County.

```
Tallyn, Joseph      age 31      Farmer              Born: England
(w)      Sarah          24      Keeping house             "
(s)      William H.      6      At home             Illinois
(s)      Arthur H.       2        "    "                   "
(s)      Edwin M.    4 mo's.      "    "                   "
```

****

The 1870 and 1880 US Census for the county lists the family residing on a farm a short distance from the town of Benson. In 1880 Joseph (age 51) is listed as having bronchitis.

Around 1890 Joseph and Sarah left the farm to retire in Benson. The 1900 US Census:Woodford Co.,Illinois lists them as follows:

```
Tallyn, Joseph   age 71  B. Apr. 1829 Married 34 yrs.  Retired Farmer
(w) Susania          66  B. Dec. 1833    "     "   "
```

****

On this census Joseph and Sarah indicate they came to the US in 1850. Sarah actually came in 1851. Both indicate they and their parents were born in England.

Joseph Tallyn died, April 19, 1902, age 73, Benson, Illinois. His obituary indicates he had a stroke (apoplexy) shortly before his death. Sarah A. (Daniel) Tallyn died, April 17, 1904 short of her 71st birthday. Both are buried Benson Cemetery, Woodford County, Illinois. Ten children were born to the marriage.

The 1880 US Census:Woodford County, Illinois:

```
Tallyn, Joseph   age 57   Farming       (Bronchitis)   Born: England
       Sarah         46   Keeping House                      "
       William       26   Farming                       Illinois
       Arthur H.     22   Farming                            "
       Edwin         20   Farming                            "
       Ella          18   At Home                            "
       Lizzie        16    "    "                            "
       Irene         14    "    "                            "
       Newton O.     10    "    "                            "
       Alice          7    "    "                            "
       Louis          1    "    "                            "
```

****

Missing is Newton Elmore Tallyn who died in infancy (1868)

Family Record.

MISCELLANEOUS.

Joseph Tallyn was born April 16th 1829

Sarah A Daniels was born December 28th 1833

We where Married March 31st 1855

William Henery Tallyn was born January 26th 1856

Arthur Herbert Tallyn was born July 19th 1857

Edwin Maurice Tallyn was born November 16th 1859

Ella Francies Tallyn was born December 1st 1861

Lizzie Eva Tallyn was born February 12th 1864

Sarah Irene Tallyn was born June 8th 1866

Newton Elmore Tallyn was born September 10th And died September 26th 1868 Aged two Weeks

Newton Oscar Tallyn was born August 21st 1869

Alice Agusta Tallyn was born Augusta 5th 1872

Lewis Litsen Tallyn was born August 5th 1878

Children and Descendants of Joseph and Sarah A.
(Daniel) Tallyn

I. William Henry Tallyn: 1856-1950)

   William was born near Kickapoo (Peoria Co.),Illinois January 28, 1856.
He grew up and obtained his education in the schools of nearby Clayton
Township of Woodford County, Illinois. At Wenona, Illinois William
married (May 12/17(?), 1911) Alice Mabel Ellison. Mabel, the daughter
of George and Catherine (Duck) Ellison, was born March 27,1879. She
was born in England. The family came to America in 1880.
   William settled in Wenona in the early 'nineties. He was a grain
dealer and successful business man of the area. He was a member of
the Methodist Church. William Henry Tallyn died May 26, 1950. At the
time he was Wenona's oldest resident (age 94). Alice Mabel (Ellison)
died September 8,1974 age 95. They are buried Wenona Cemetery, Wenona
(Marshall Co.), Illinois. Their 4 children were born in Wenona.

   A. William Edwin Tallyn: Edwin was born January 20,1912. On Sept.
4, 1937 at Toluca, Illinois Edwin married Lydia Marie Leonelli. She
is the daughter of Dominic and Angelina (Melchiori) Leonelli and was
born April 25, 1916 at Toluca, Ill. Edwin, now retired, was a teacher
at Fremont High School, Oakland, California. He enjoys genealogy
and has spent time in England tracing ancestors on the Tallyn and
Ellison family lines. He is a major contributor to this section of
this work.
   The family presently makes its home at Walnut Creek, California.
2 Children

      1. Karen Susanne Tallyn: Karen was born January 15, 1939 in
Laurium, Michigan. On June 16, 1962 in San Francisco, California
Karen married (1st) John Beggin. John died February 10,1963,Alameda
Naval Air Base (Calif). In Palo Alto, California Karen married(2nd)
Peter Barton Dahl on July 7,1964.

      2. Robert Bernard Tallyn: Robert was born January 11,1941 in
Delano, California. On September 1, 1972 at Bakersfield (Kern Co.),
California Robert married Susan Moore. They make their home at Ojai,
California.

   B. Ronald Ellison Tallyn: Ronald was born June 15, 1913. At Mani-
tou Springs, Colorado he married(May 8,1941) Lucile Dahlsten. She is
the daughter of Carl Algot Eben and Emma Cecelia Mabel(Krantz) Dahlsten. Lucile was born March 9, 1918 in Smolan, Kansas. The family
makes its home at Wenona, Illinois. Four children were born to the
marriage. Three appear to have been still born. Data for two is incomplete.

      1. Infant Tallyn: B. Wenona, Illinois
                        D.   "   "
      2. Infant Tallyn: B. Wenona, Illinois
                        D.   "   "

3. William Craig Tallyn: William was born May 1,1947 (probably Wenona, Ill.). On June 23, 1973, at Sycamore, Illinois, William married Kay Lucille Schiniski.

4. <u>Mary Tallyn</u>:   B. April 3, 1952 Wenona, Ill.
                         D. April 3, 1952 Wenona, Ill.

****

C. <u>Alice Marsha Tallyn</u>:   Alice, the daughter of William Henry and Mabel (Ellison) Tallyn, was born January 1,1919. She died February 25, 1919. She is buried Wenona, Illinois.

****

D. <u>George Bernard Tallyn</u>:   George, the son of William H. and Mabel (Ellison) Tallyn, was born April 12, 1921. On September 1, 1949, at Wenona (Marshall Co.), Illinois, he married Helen Margaret Burgess. She was born in Wenona June 30, 1930 and is the daughter of Robert C. and Florence (Day) Burgess. George and Helen make their home in So. San Francisco, Calif.   5 Children

1. <u>Marsha Lucinda Tallyn</u>: Marsha was born September 24, 1951, Berkeley, California.

2. <u>Taffy Elizabeth Tallyn</u>: · Taffy was born in Pittsburg, California, October 21,1952. In Saratoga, California she married (April 24,1976) Peter Handy.

3. <u>John Burgess Tallyn</u>: John was born in Walnut Creek, California, March 12, 1954. On December 23, 1973 at Saratoga, California John married Patricia Matson. John and Patricia make their home in (So.)San Francisco, California.

4. <u>Terry Ann Tallyn</u>: Terry was born in San Francisco,Calif., February 23,1957.

Twins

5. <u>Thomas Henry Tallyn</u>: Thomas was born February 23, 1957 in San Francisco, California.

****

Notes of Genealogical Interest

One reference indicates Mabel (Ellison) Tallyn was born at Swindon, England. Another notes she was born at Cricklade, England.

The author is indebted to Edwin Tallyn of Walnut Creek, California who made his records on the family of William Henry and Mabel(Ellison) Tallyn available for use in this document.

II. Arthur Herbert Tallyn: (1857-1939) [1]

Arthur was born on the Tallyn farm near Benson, July 19,1857. In Benson, on July 9, 1888 Arthur married Anna Maria Heiken. Anna, the daughter of Sjut and Jabe Maria (Wertz) Heiken, was born, April 22, 1867 Ostfriesland, Germany. The Heiken family came to America in 1881, (See Heiken family in appendix for additional information).
Verna (Tallyn) Herbst, the daughter of Arthur and Anna notes:

"...Before he married, my father attended Valparaiso University (Indiana) for one year. He was a member of Modern Woodmen of America. He served Clayton township (Woodford Co.,Ill.) as Supervisor in 1909. He was an elected deacon of the Benson Baptist Church. Arthur was one of the first in the county to own a car, a Stanley Steamer."

Arthur is credited for inventing a manually operated cutting tool for cutting weeds, straw and hay.It was patented in the United States and Canada in 1916 and 1917, respectively.
Arthur was 18 when a fierce tornado swept across Roanake and Clayton townships, October 19,1875. Verna recalls her father saying:

".......Many houses were destroyed. Strong winds carried some of our chickens away for a mile. Straw stems were driven into fence posts...."

Arthur, a life-long resident and farmer of Woodford County, died, July 5, 1939...just <u>14</u> days prior to his 82nd. birthday. Anna Maria (Heiken) Tallyn died, May 1 (2?), 1951. Both are buried Benson Cemetery, Woodford County, Illinois. 5 children
The <u>1900 US Census for Clayton Township of Woodford County, Illinois:</u> lists the family as follows:

<u>Tallyn, A.H.</u>	B. July 1857	age 43	married 11yrs	Farmer	Born: Illinois
(w) Anna	Apr. 1867	33	(To US in 1881)		Germany
(s) Bruce	Apr. 1889	11	At home		Illinois
(s) Sidney	Oct. 1892	8	" "		"
(s) Chester	May 1898	2	" "		"

****

Daughters Ethel and Verna Tallyn were born after 1900 when the census was taken.

1. Bruce Edward Tallyn: (1889-1961)

Bruce was born, April 20, 1889 on the family farm near Benson. He was a graduate of Benson High School. He gave an oration on <u>Public Opinion</u> at the 1906 Commencement held at the Benson Opera House. He was a member of the Benson Band (1904). He was a student at Eureka College (Eureka,Ill.). Bruce and his brother Sidney owned and operated a furniture-hardware store and undertaking business in Benson and Minonk of Woodford County.

---

1 The author is indebted to Verna (Tallyn) Herbst who made her notes on the family of Arthur and Anna (Heiken)Tallyn available for use in this segment.

64

A complimentary advertising handout reads:

****

COMPLIMENTS OF TALLYN BROS.

Dealers in Hardware, Stoves, Tinware,Silverplate Ware
Cream Separators, Granite and Delftware
Also Oil and Gasoline Stores....
Benson, Ill.

****

Bruce left the furniture store and funeral business around 1939 when he moved to Eureka (Woodford Co.),Illinois. He served (2 years) as Sheriff and Deputy Sheriff of Woodford County and Justice of the Peace for six years. He was a member of the Benson Baptist Chruch and later, the Eureka Christian Church. He was a member of Mohammed Shrine and Scottish Rite Consistory of Peoria and Modern Woodmen of America.[1]

On June 14, 1911, in Benson, Illinois, Bruce married, Lena Woltzen. Lena, the daughter of Albert and Ella (Johnson) Woltzen, was born,July 12,1889, Benson (Woodford Co.),Illinois. Lena attended Illinois Weslyn, Normal,Illinois. She taught piano for many years. Lena was a Past Worthy Matron and a member of Woman's Club of Benson and Eureka. Bruce and Lena made their home in Benson and later Eureka. *

Bruce Edward Tallyn died, September 3, 1961, age 82. Lena (Woltzen) Tallyn died in Portales (Roosevelt Co.),New Mexico, October 7, 1973. Both are buried, Benson Cemetery, Woodford Co.,Illinois. 2 children

A. Chauncy Wright Tallyn: Chauncy was born in Benson, February 16, 1918. He married Geneva E. Shields. Geneva, the daughter of James and Anna (Malone) Shields, was born, March 18, 1918. They make their home at Tuscon, Arizona. 3 children

    1. Maureen   Tallyn: B. September 4, 1944 Peoria (Peoria Co.),Ill.

    2. Georgia   Tallyn: B. September 11,1945   "   "   "   "

    3. Bruce   Tallyn: B. February 9,1947 Bloomington, Illinois

In April of 1966 Bruce married,Joan Hock of Benson, Illinois. They were married in Benson. 2 children

    a. Bruce Tallyn: B. 1966
    b. Chris Tallyn: B. 1969
    *****

B. Joyce Ethelyn Tallyn: Joyce was born, February 9, 1923, Benson, Woodford Co.,Illinois. She took nursing training at Evanston Hospital School of Nursing, Northwestern University (Illinois). She received her B.S. Degree from Eureka College. She did graduate work at Indiana University, East New Mexico University and University of New Mexico. Joyce has worked in a wide range of hospital and health-related settings in

---

1 1900 US Census:Woodford Co. (Clayton Twp.),Illinois
    Woltzen, Ella B. March 1862 age 38 (widow) Born: Illinois
          Sena B.   1884   15   "   Illinois
          Lena B.   1886   13   "   "
               ****

* Bruce died in Benson, Illinois

Ohio and New Mexico. For the past 13 years she has been Health Occupations Instructor and School Nurse at Portales H.S., Portales, New Mexico.

On December 24, 1947, in Eureka, Illinois, Joyce married, Robert Lyle Hagan. Robert, the son of James Jackson and Carrie (Lyle) Hagan, was born, March 1903, Kewanee, Illinois. Dr. Hagan is Dean Emeritus, College of Communicative Arts and Sciences, East New Mexico University. 5 children

1. <u>Colette Nadine Hagan</u>: Colette was born, March 9, 1949, Cleveland, Ohio. She is a graduate of the University of Nevada (M.A. Degree). She worked as a Reading Specalist, Las Vegas H.S. On February 18, 1974 Colette married John Welsing. 1 child

a. <u>Charisse Monica Welsing</u>: B. March 23, 1977

2. <u>Adrienne Joyce Hagan</u>: Adrienne was born, March 28, 1951, Bloomington, Indiana. She has a M.S. Degree from West Texas State. She worked as a Speech Pathologist at the University of New Orleans. She presently works in this same capacity for the Grand Junction Schools of Grand Junction, Colorado.

On December 17, 1977, Ardienne married Dan Chun. Dan is a graduate of the University of Mississippi (B.S. Degree). He is with DuPont Chemical Co., Grand Junction, Colorado.

3. <u>Denise Ellen Hagan</u>: Denise was born in Bloomington, Indiana, June 17, 1954. She is a graduage of East New Mexico University (B.S. Degree) and is presently a doctoral candidate in Oceanography at Texas A and M.

4. <u>James Lyle Hagan</u>: James was born December 18, 1955, Portales, New Mexico. He completed his studies in Civil Engineering at New Mexico State at Las Cruces, New Mexico.

5. <u>Robert Bruce Hagan</u>: Bob was born, November 22, 1962, Portales, N.M. He is a senior at Portales, H.S.

****

2. <u>Sidney Elmo Tallyn</u>:(1892-1949)

Sidney was born on the Tallyn farm near Benson, October 10, 1892. He was a member of the Benson Band. He was a 1910 graduate of Benson H.S. On June 3, 1910 he gave an oration on: <u>The Men of Illinois</u> marking the commencement program at the Benson Opera House. [1]
On June 2, 1914, at Benson, Sidney married, Elsie Theresa Learned. Elsie, the daughter of Frank Elmo and Martha (Mattie) Ellen (Huxtable) Learned, was born in Benson, January 28, 1894, (See Huxtable Family in Appendix). Sidney attended Illinois Wesleyan University (Bloomington, Ill.) and Barnes Mortuary College (Chicago, Ill.). In 1914 Sidney and his brother, Bruce, started a furniture-hardware store and a under-taking business. The February 18, 1918 edition of <u>The Benson Bee</u> contained the following advertisements:

S.E. Tallyn: Local Agent For Stark Pianos

---
[1] Elsie was a 1910 graduate of Benson H.S. On the commencement program she spoke on: <u>The Spirit That Wins.</u>

****

NEW FURNITURE AT TALLYNS: COME AND SEE....
.....We Carry a Full Line of Fixtures and Electrical
Appliances...........
Furniture, Plugs and Undertaking
                    S.E. Tallyn   Benson, Ill.

****

In 1920 the family moved to Minonk, Illinois. Sidney dropped the
furniture-hardware store but kept the undertaking business. Verna
(Tallyn) Herbst notes that Sidney was a member of the Baptist Church of
Minonk, Mohammed Shrine, Elks,Modern Woodmen of America, Minonk Chamber
of Commerce and Minonk Fire Department. He was the Coroner of Woodford Co.,
for 16 years. The post (Coroner) was political and Sidney was the only
Republican to win in a Democratic landslide in 1936.
    Sidney Elmo Tallyn died, July 13,1949(Minonk, Ill.) just two months
prior to his 57th birthday.. Elsie Theresa (Learned) Tallyn died, May
7, 1957, age 63, Minonk, Illinois. Both are buried Benson Cemetery,Wood-
ford Co., Ill. 2 children

    A. Harrison Learned Tallyn: Harrison was born in Benson, April 9, 1916.
He was drafted into the US Army at Ft. Sheridan, Illinois in 1940. He went
through basic training (Field Artillery) at Camp Roberts, California. He was
stationed at Ft. Benning, Georgia and Seoul, Korea. Master Sgt. Tallyn was
discharged (honorable) in 1945.
    Harrison took over the family funeral business in 1949 which he operated
until 1960. Since then he has been a representative with Metropolitan Life
Insurance Company, Claremont, California. He is a member of Masons, Consistory
and Shrines (inactive). His leisure time activities include fishing.
    In Nashua (Cickasaw Co.),Iowa, Harrison married (June 28,1939, Edith.
Charlene Kimpling. She is the daughter of Ralph Van Hove and Ethelyn (McCully)
Kimpling. Edith was born, January 28, 1918, LaRose (Marshall Co.), Illinois.
She attended (2yrs) Illinois State University (Normal, Ill.) and Chaffey
College (Calif.).and San Bernadino College (2 yrs.). She is Director of
Food Services Upland School Dist. (Calif.). She is a member of San Bernadino
Co. Food Service and the Altruna Club. Her leisure activities include sewing.
1 child
    a. Laura Jeanne Tallyn: Laura was born, January 25, 1950, Streator,
Illinois. She attended Cal Poly University (2 yrs.). Laura, a single woman,
is Title Officer for Title Insurance Co.,Burbank, California.

****

    B. Elizabeth Ann Tallyn: Elizabeth, the daughter of Sidney and Elsie
(Learned) Tallyn, was born, March 29, 1918, Benson, Illinois. Elizabeth, a
single woman, died, February 4,1938, just a few days prior to her 20th.
birthday. She is buried Benson Cemetery, Woodford County, Illinois.

*****

    3. Chester Arthur Tallyn: Chester was born on the Arthur Tallyn
farm near Benson, May 8, 1898. He was a member of the Benson Band (1904).
He served in the 23rd. Signal Corp. (1942-43) during World War II. He
received an Honorable Discharge. He was a member of the Baptist Church and
American Legion of Benson. Chester A. Tallyn, a single man,died,December
27,1944.

*****

4. Ethel Tallyn: Ethel, the daughter of Arthur and Anna (Heiken) Tallyn, was born on the family farm near Benson, August 30, 1904. She was the first girl born in the second generation descendants of Joseph and Sarah (Daniel) Tallyn. In Gary (Lake Co.), Indiana, Ethel married (May 4, 1931) Truman Overby. Truman, the son of Noah Clarence and Nellie(Manz) Overby, was born, September 26, 1903, Carrolton, Illinois.* Truman died, March 6, 1954. He is buried Gary, Indiana. Ethel continues to make her home in Gary. 1 child

> A. Truman Tallyn Overby: Truman was born in Gary, Indiana, June 4, 1933. He is a graduate of Gary H.S. and Indiana University (at Bloomington). He has been a police officer in Gary for the past 19 years. On August 8, 1958 Truman married, Lillian Fernandez. Their two children were born in Gary, Indiana.
>
> > a. Kathy Overby: B. October 13, 1960.
> >
> > b. Michael Overby: B. January 9, 1962

****

5. Verna Annette Tallyn: Verna, the daughter of Arthur H. and Anna (Heiken) Tallyn, was born on the family farm near Benson, November 16, 1906. She is a graduate of Benson H.S. She attended Shurtleff College (1 yr.) and Illinois State University at Normal, Ill. She taught grades 3 and 4 in Benson (1926-34) and at Washington Grade School (Washington, Ill.) between 1944-1964.
   On December 24, 1934, in San Antonio, Texas, Verna married Frank Herbst. Frank, the son of Earnest and Magdalena (Blunier) Herbst, was born, April 12, 1900, Roanoke (Woodford Co.),Illinois.
   Verna is a member of the Washington Methodist Church, Eastern Star, Garden and Woman's Clubs. She is a member of Royal Neighbors of America and Tazwell County Retired Teacher's Association. Her leisure time activities include a interest in genealogy.
   Frank Herbst died, September 5, 1972 age 72. He is buried, Benson Cemetery, Woodford Co.,Illinois. Verna (Tallyn) Herbst continues to make her home at Washington, Illinois. 1 child.

> A. Kay Herbst: Kay was born, Jan. 20, 1935, McAllen (HidalgoCo.),Texas. She is a graduate of Washington H.S. and class co-valedictorian. She has a B.S. Degree from Bradley University and M.A. Degree from Stout University (Menomonee, Wisconsin). She plays the saxaphone, piano and organ... and has a interest in social work.
> On June 24 /25(?), 1961, in Washington, Illinois Kay married Kenneth Helms. Ken is the son of Lawrence Nelson and Dorothy (Henderson) Helms. He was born, January 27, 1936, Peoria (Peoria Co.), Illinois.   3 children
>
> > 1.Jeffrey Helms: B. March 30, 1962   Chicago (Cook Co.), Ill.
> >
> > 2. Nathan Helms: B. Sept. 25, 1966   Toronto (Ontario),Canada
> >
> > 3. Drew Helms: B. Nov. 21, 1968   Peoria (Peoria Co.), Ill.

****

*Nancy(Nellie) Manz b. July 14,1883 Green Co.,Ill. d. Apr.30, 1971 Toledo, Ohio.Noah Clarence Overby b. Sept. 23,1877 Pratt Co.Ill. d. July 3,1931 Green Co.Ill. They married Dec.10,1902 Green Co.,Ill.

III. Edwin Maurice Tallyn: (1859-1918)

Edwin, the son of Joseph and Sarah A. (Daniel) Tallyn was born November 19,1859 near Benson of Woodford County, Illinois. He grew up and obtained his education in the county. In July of 1888 Edwin purchased 240 acres in the S.W. quarter and the West half of the S.E. quarter of Section 35 of Clayton Twp. of Woodford County. The farm was originally owned by Adolphus W. and Mary A. (Diehl) Forney. Adolphus purchased the land from a U.S. Government Land Agent on March 28,1854. This original sale is recorded on certificate 14,875 and signed by President Franklin Pierce, March 1, 1855.

On January 14,1891 in Benson, Illinois Edwin married Sarah Margaret McCue. Sarah the daughter of Cyrus and Frances (Glenn) McCue, was born October 30,1869 on the McCue homestead near Afton (Nelson Co.),Virginia. (See McCue and Jones Families in Appendix for additional data)

Edwin and Sarah moved to the newly acquired farm-home March 1, 1891. Edwin built a new home equipped with the latest conveniences in 1910.The home (freshly painted) stands today. Edwin, a farmer and stockman, served as assessor and tax collector of Clayton Township. He was a member of the Clayton Baptist Church since 1888. He was a major stockholder in the First State Bank of Benson.

Edwin Maurice Tallyn suffered from a severe attack of pneumonia some nine days before his death, Tuesday, February 12,1918 at 2:30 P.M. There is indication Edwin was troubled earlier with pneumonia in 1910. His father suffered from bronchitis.

Sarah Margaret (McCue) Tallyn lived out her life on the farm. She was an active member of the Benson Baptist Church. Sarah died in Brokaw Hospital at Normal, Illinois, July 27,1963 at age 93. Edwin and Sarah are buried Clayton Cemetery of Woodford County, Ill. Their five children were all born in the County.

The 1900 US Census for Woodford County (Clayton Twp.),Illinois,lists the family as follows:

Tallyn, Edward	b. Nov. 1859 age 40	Farming	Born: Illinois
(w) Sallie	b. Oct. 1869 30		Virginia
(s) DeWitt	b. Nov. 1891 8	At School	Illinois
(s) Harold	b. Dec. 1895 4	At Home	"
(s) Brainard	b. Sept.1897 2	" "	"
(s) Joseph	b. June 1900	less than 1 month	"

****

The census was taken June 18,1900. It is of interest to note Joseph is listed as less than a month old. Another source indicates he was born April 16,1900. If so he would have been two months old(2/12) at the time the census was taken. Son Franklin M. Tallyn is not listed on the census. He was born later in 1902.

A. Dewitt Edwin Tallyn:(1891-1960)

Dewitt was born November 15, 1891. He was a 1907 graduate of Benson H.S. He was a skilled mechanic. He took over the management of the farm after the death of his father in 1918. He was a life member of the H.H. Franklin Club, American Forestry Association, National Rifle Assoc. of America and Antique Automobile Club of America. He was a collector of Franklin motor cars. Dewitt, a single man, made his home on the Tallyn farm near Benson.

Dewitt Edwin Tallyn died April 25,1960 at age 68. He is buried Clayton Township Cemetery of Woodford County. No Descendants.

69

B. William Harold Tallyn: (1895-1978)

Harold was born December 8,1895. To some he was affectionately known as "Bill". He spent his youth helping on the family farm. He attended Eagle School,a one room country school, where he obtained his elementary education. At age 15 he was one of the youngest to graduate from Benson H.S. He was class valedictorian and his address to the graduates was titled, "Success". In 1915 he enrolled in Shurtleff Academy and later the college at Alton, Illinois. His studies were interrupted by the onset of World War I. He enlisted (age 21) at Campt Dodge, Des Moines, Iowa. At Camp Pike (Little Rock, Arkansas) he trained to become a engineer. On August 24,1918 his company, Co. E of the 312th Engineers, sailed for Europe. He served in France. On July 16, 1919, at Camp Grant (Illinois), Sgt. William H. Tallyn was given an Honorable Discharge.

In the Fall of 1919 he resumed his studies at Shurtleff College. He received a B.S. Degree in 1921. The year 1922 was marked by his enrollment in Harvard University and his marriage (Sept. 9,1922) to Etta Esther Jones. Etta, the daughter of Francis Louis and Anne Rebecca(Bailey) Jones, was born near El Paso, Illinois, September 9,1895.[1] She was a graduate of El Paso H.S. and a 1920 graduate of Shurtleff College (B.S. Degree: Home Economics). She was a Supervisor and Instructor in Home Economics (1920-22) for the East St.Louis grade schools.

Harold and Etta first made their home at Cambridge and later Ewing, Illinois. During this time (1924-25) Harold taught Science and Math. at Ewing College and completed his M.S. Degree in Chemistry (1925) at the University of Illinois (Champaign-Urbana).

In 1925 Harold , Etta and their infant son, Edwin, travelled to Cheney in the State of Washington. Harold accepted a teaching appointment at the state college there (Eastern Washington State College) which included teaching chemistry and physics.

His professional career spanned 32 years. He advanced from the rank of Instructor to Professor of Chemistry. He was a life member of the American Assoc....for the Advancement of Science. He was a 50 year member and Past Master of the Cheney Masonic Temple and since 1949 a Shriner, El Katif Temple of Spokane, Washington.

Etta Esther (Jones) Tallyn died, August 22,1954, after a long and difficult struggle with diabetes. She is buried Riverside Memorial Park, Spokane, Washington. Harold continued to make his home in Cheney until he retired....in 1956. He worked as a mine chemist , for about a year, in the Metalline Falls area of Idaho. He lived out his life in Southern California. His many interests included rock and stamp collecting. He was a collector of Franklin motor cars. In California he made his home in Manhattan Beach. William Harold Tallyn died, July 5, 1978, Torrance (Harbor General Hospital),California.Memorial services were held in Cheney, Washington, July 12, 1978. He is buried Riverside Memorial Park, Spokane, Washington. 3 Children

---

1 See McCue and Jones Families in Appendix

70

1. Edwin Francis Tallyn:

Edwin was born March 1,1924, Champaign (Champaign Co.),Illinois. He is a 1941 graduate of Cheney H.S. (Cheney, Washington) and class valedictorian. He attended (1941-1943) Eastern Washington State College (at Cheney). He has a B.S. Degree (1947) and M.S. Degree (1949) from Washington State University (Pullman, Wash.). He served in the US Army (1944-46) during World War II.

Ed is a member of Sigma Chi Fraternity,Alpha Phi Omega, Alpha Chi Sigma and Sigma Tau honary societies.He is also an Eagle Scout.

On April 15,1950,in Martinez California, Edwin married Lois Helen Kresbach. Lois, the daughter of John Albert and Edith Frances(Coleman) Kresbach, was born in Fargo (Cass Co.),North Dakota, December 15, 1925. Lois is a 1943 graduate of Fargo H.S. She has a B.S.Degree (1948) from North Dakota State University (Fargo). She did graduate work at the University of California at Berkeley. She taught (1949-50) Home Economics at Martinez Jr. High School at Martinez, Calif. She is a member of Kappa Delta sorority.

Ed and Lois first made their home in Martinez and later Concord, Calif. In Concord Ed served on the California Park and Recreation Commission and Concord Planning Commission. During their years in California Ed, a chemist, worked for Phillips Petroleum Co.He presently works for the company at the Kansas City, Kansas facility. Ed and Lois make their home in nearby Lenexa, Kansas.   3 children

A. Catherine Ann Tallyn: Cathy was born August 24,1951, Oakland (Alameda Co.), California. She is a 1969 graduate of Carondelet H.S. of Concord, Calif. She has an Associate of Arts Degree (1971) from Diablo Valley College and a B.A. Degree (1973) from San Jose State University. She is a member of Sigma Delta Chi, Kappa Tau Alpha and Theta Sigma Phi societies. She is a First Class Scout (GSA). Cathy is presently on the staff of Contra Costa Times Newspaper of Walnut Creek, California.

On October 20,1979 at Queen of All Saints Church of Concord, California Catherine Ann Tallyn married Benjamin Joel Reed.

B. Deborah Joan Tallyn: Deborah was born in Oakland (Alameda Co.), California, May 17, 1953. She is a 1971 graduate of Carondelet H.S. and a 1973 graduate of Diablo Valley Junior College (A.A. Degree). She has a B.A. Degree (1976) from San Francisco State University where she graduated Magna Cum Laude. She is a First Class Scout (GSA). Debby, a single woman, is presently with Chevron Research of Richmond, California.

c. Edwin Francis Tallyn (Jr.):   Edwin was born April 8, 1955, Walnut Creek (Contra Costa Co.),California. He is a 1973 graduate of De-Lasalle H.S. (Concord, Calif.) and a 1976 graduate (A.A.Degree) of Diablo Valley Junior College.He has a B.S. Degree (1979) from Humbolt State University (Arcata,Calif.). Ed, a single man, holds the rank of Eagle Scout (BSA).

****

The author is indebted to Mrs. Edwin Tallyn of Lenexa, Kansas for her assistance with the family of Edwin F. and Lois (Kresbach)Tallyn.

2. William Harold Tallyn (Jr.):

Bill, the son of William and Etta(Jones) Tallyn, was born June 8,1928 in Cheney (Spokane Co.),Washington. He is a graduate of Cheney H.S. and Eastern Washington State Collge where he earned a B.A. Degree and a M.A.Degree (1958) in education and science.

Sgt. Bill Tallyn saw action in Korea during the Korean War. Since 1955 he has taught in the secondary schools of Spokane, Washington. In addition to his regular classroom duties he teaches Driver Education and Training.

In Spokane, Washington, William H. Tallyn (Jr.) married (Aug. of 1956) Lee Ann Koch. Lee Ann, the daughter of Solomon and Mary Freda(Mashburn) Koch,was born in Spokane, May 2, 1937. She obtained her elementary and secondary education in the public schools of Spokane. She completed her undergraduate studies at Eastern Washington State University at Cheney and is presently engaged in graduate studies in Geology at Eastern. Lee Ann played violin several seasons with the Spokane Symphony.

The family makes their home in the original Tallyn homeplace in Cheney, Washington.   3 children

A. Kristin Lin Tallyn: Kris was born May 8, 1959, Spokane, Wash. She is a 1977 graduate of Cheney H.S. She plays the flute. Since high school she has studied Bookkeeping. Her Fall 1979 plans include studies in Early Childhood Education at Eastern Washington State University.

B. Karen Elaine Tallyn: Karen,the daughter of William and Lee Ann (Koch) Tallyn, was born, January 13,1961, Spokane, Washington..She died January 1, 1962 Spokane, Washington. Karen Elaine Tallyn is buried Riverside Memorial Park, Spokane, Washington.

C. Dale Russell Tallyn: Dale was born March 31, 1962 in Spokane, Washington. He is a student at Cheney H.S.His interests include Theatre, cooking(pizza) and helping his father remodel and restore the Tallyn home at Cheney.

****

3. Annetta Jean Tallyn:

Annetta, the daughter of William H. and Etta E.(Jones) Tallyn, was born January 19,1933 Cheney., Washington. She completed her elementary and secondary education in the schools of Cheney, Washington. At Cheney H.S. she was an honor student and class valedictorian. She was a student at Eastern Washington State Collge at Cheney. In 1959 she was awarded the B.A. Degree (Education) from Long Beach State College (Long Beach, Calif.). Since graduation she has been a teacher (elementary) with the Torrance Unified School District of Torrance, California.

On June 8, 1952, in Cheney (Spokane Co.),Washington Annetta married Donn Lee Cochran. He is the son of Glen and Marie (Sheffer) Cochran. He was born May 2, 1928 in Colfax (Whitman Co.),Washington. He is a 1947 graduate of Walla Walla H.S. (Walla Walla, Wash.). He is

veteran of World War II (US Navy:1946-48). He is a graduate (1952) of
Eastern Washington State College (B.A.Degree:Education), University of
California at Los Angeles (M.A.Degree 1960) and (Ed.D.1965: Education
and Psychology). Upon graduation he joined the faculty of the Graduate
School of Public Health(Division of Behavioral Science & Health Edu-
cation)at UCLA and held the rank of Assistant Professor of Public
Health. In addition to professional publications he has written and
published five works on genealogy.

    Annetta and Donn make their home in Manhattan Beach, California.
Their leisure time activities include camping, beach activities and
genealogy. 3 children

    A. Kenneth Lee Cochran: Ken was born March 13,1953 in Portland
(Multnomah Co.),Oregon. He completed his elementary studies in the
public schools of Manhattan Beach. He is a 1971 graduate of Westchester
H.S. (Westchester, Calif.). He attended El Camino Jr. College of
Torrance, Calif. Ken, a single man is an Assistant Manager with a
large department store chain (FedMart). His interests include camping,
photography, softball and working with ecology- orientated groups.
He presently makes his home in Winnetka of the San Fernando Valley
(Los Angles Co.),California.

    B. Garry Lee Cochran: Garry was born October 28, 1955 in Portland
(Multnomah Co.),Oregon. He completed his studies in the public schools of
Manhattan Beach and Westchester, California. He was a 1973 graduate of
Aviation H.S. He completed two years of study at El Camio Junior College.
    Garry was active in several collegiate, church and civic choral
groups. As a member of the Southen California based group Musical Americans
he toured the Near East (1976) and South America (1975).His most recent
employment was with Ampex Corporation of El Segundo, California.
    Garry Lee Cochran, a single man,died of an auto accident August
6, 1977. His place of inurnment is Pacific Crest Cemetery, Redondo Beach,
California.

    C. Karen Lynn Cochran: Karen was born May 20, 1968 Redondo Beach,
California. She spent the first three years of life at Playa Del Rey
(Los Angeles Co.),California where the family lived. In 1971 the family
returned to Manhattan Beach. Karen attended Ladera Elementary School of
Manhattan Beach. She is presently attending the sixth grade at Center
Intermediate School of Manhattan Beach. She plays flute in the school
band. She is a Girl Scout (GSA). Her interests include camping, roller
skating, swimming and reading.

****

C.Brainard Olin Tallyn: (1897-1963)

    Brainard, the son of Edwin M. and Sarah M.(McCue)Tallyn, was born
near Benson (Woodford Co.), Illinois, September 8, 1897. He grew up and
obtained his education in the public schools of the County. He was a
graduate of the Sweeny Automobile School (1917-18).
    In Chicago (Cook Co.),Illinois he completed a course in Aviation
Mechanics. In Flanigan (Livingston Co.),Illinois, Brainard married
Minnie Elizabeth Hornman. She was born October 9, 1901 in Minonk, Ill.
    Brainard O. Tallyn died, April 16,1963 at age 63. After his death
Minnie continued to make her home at Las Cruces, New Mexico. She may
now make her home at Flanigan, Illinois. 1 child

1. <u>Audrey Jean Tallyn</u>:   Audrey was born December 1,1926 in Pontiac, Illinois. She married Ray Lunsford. They first made their home in Las Cruces, N.M. and later Big Springs, Texas.   2 children

      a. <u>Ray Lunsford</u>:   (No additional data)

      b. <u>Greg Lunsford</u>:   (No additional data)

****

D. <u>Joseph Cyrus Tallyn</u>: (1900-1964)

      Joseph the son of Edwin M. and Sarah M. (McCue) Tallyn, was born April 16, 1900 near Benson (Woodford Co.), Illinois. (The <u>1900 US Census for Woodford County</u> indicates he was born in June of 1900) Joseph was a farmer, dairyman and poultry raiser. He grew up and spent much of his life on the Tallyn farm near Benson.
      On April 20,1930 in Nashua (Chickasaw Co.),Iowa, Joseph married Leona Talena Hohl. Leona was born April 20, 1908 in El Paso (Woodford Co.), Illinois. She is the daughter of Ernst and Sena (Sandhorst) Hohl.
      Joseph was a member of the Benson Baptist Church. Joseph Cyrus Tallyn died January 28,1964 at age 63 (St. James Hospital:Pontiac, Ill.). He is buried Clayton Cemetery of Woodford County, Ill. Leona (Hohl) Tallyn makes her home in Minonk, Illinois.   3 children

      1. <u>Joseph Junior Tallyn</u>:   Joe was born October 25,1936 in Woodford Co.,Illinois. He was educated in the schools of the County . Rev. Joe Tallyn has a B.A. Degree in Religious Education. He is presently Executive Director for Youth For Christ in Huntsville, Alabama. He recently received an award marking 20 years of outstanding service in Y.F.C. He enjoys and participates in a wide variety of sports.
      On November 28, 1958 in Fredonia (Wilson Co.),Kansas Joe married Donna Louise Cook. Donna, the daughter of Arthur Carroll and Rosa Anna (Brandenberger) Cook, was born August 2,1937, Wichita (Sedgewick Co.), Kansas. Donna is a Registered Nurse (R.N.) and is presently working on a degree in music.   The   family   resides in Huntsville, Alabama. 2 children

            a.<u>Steven Joseph Tallyn</u>:   Steven was born December 31,1963 in Milwaukee, Wisconsin.

            b. <u>Bruce Franklin Tallyn</u>:   Bruce was born in Pecatonia, Ill., February 17, 1966.

      2. <u>Donna Lee Tallyn</u>:   Donna, the daughter of Joseph C. and Leona (Hohl) Tallyn, was born August 22,1939 in Benson(Woodford Co.), Illinois. In Benson she married (Aug. 22,1962) Ronald C. Peterson (b. Sept. 21,1938:Grantsburg, Wisc.), the son of Carl G. and Grace(Anderson) Peterson. Donna and Ronald are graduates of Greenville College(Ill.) with degrees (B.A.) in social studies-psychology and math-science,res—pectively.They make their home in Lombard, Ill. where Donna is in real estate and Ronald is Physical Dist. Manager for the Gliddon Div. of S.. C.M.   1 Child

            a. <u>Kyle Eric Peterson</u>:   Kyle was born February 11, 1974 in Reading (Burks Co.), Pennsylvania.

74

3. <u>Mary Anita Tallyn</u>:   Mary, the daughter of Joseph C. and Leona T. (Hohl) Tallyn, was born April 4,1943. She was born in Streator, Ill. On September 9, 1962, at the Benson Baptist Church of Benson, Illinois, she married David Alan Sheley. Alan, the son of John and Verna(Greenslate), Sheley, was born July 18, 1940 in Peoria of Peoria County, Illinois.

Mary and Alan first made their home in Peoria and later Benson. They recently moved to Bacus, Minnesota where they own and operate a resort. Their two children were born in Peoria, Illinois

      1. <u>David Alan Sheley, Jr.</u>:   B. May 29, 1963

      2. <u>Dawn Annette Sheley</u>:   B. September 17, 1965.

******

E. <u>Franklin McCue Tallyn</u>: (1902-   )

Frank was born August 12,1902 near Benson of Woodford Co.,Ill. He is a 1920 graduate of Minonk Community High School and a 1924 graduate of Shurtleff College (B.S. Degree) at Alton, Illinois. He taught and coached at Fairview, Illinois (1925-26). Since 1926 until retirement (1961) Frank was with Harris Trust and Savings Bank of Chicago. His leaisure time activities include part-time mechanic, electrician, plumber and carpenter.

On August 4, 1934 at Crown Point, Indiana Frank married Eleanor Louise Schuck. Eleanor, the daughter of George John and Viola May (Hanroth) Schuck, was born August 20, 1909 in Chicago (Cook Co.), Ill. She completed two years of business college and worked as a secretary in a patent law office. She is active in the St. Paul Community Church.

Frank and Eleanor make their home at Homewood, Illinois. Weather and time permitting Frank enjoys visiting the Tallyn farm near Benson of which he is part owner.   No Children

*****

It is of interest to note that Mrs. Donna Tallyn, wife of Joseph Junior Tallyn, was the soloist at the memorial service for Joseph C. Tallyn and DeWitt Tallyn. The program for the service for Mrs. Sarah M. (McCue) Tallyn lists Mrs. Donna Tallyn under Music.

Of Historical
Interest

Records of the Woodford County Courthouse show the following entry:

James F. Huxtable and Nora F. Huxtable, his wife, of the Village of Benson in the County of Woodford and State of Illinois for the consideration of <u>Twenty</u> Dollars, convey and Quit claim to: <u>E.M. Tallyn</u> of the <u>Township of Clayton</u> the following described Real Estate,to-wit:

    Lot number one hundred and forty one (141) on the recorded plat
    of the Benson Cemetery in the Township of Clayton

December 23, 1898

75

IV. Ella Frances Tallyn: (1861-1929)

Ella, the daughter of Joseph and Sarah A. (Daniel) Tallyn, was born December 1, 1861 near Benson of Woodford County, Illinois. On October 28, 1890 in Woodford County, Ella married Wm. Ridge. He was born September 21, 1855. [1] Ella and William first made their home near Minonk, Illinois. At some point prior to 1914 the family moved to Rockwell City, Iowa. The farming community is located about 25 miles W. by S.W. of Fort Dodge. Letters of correspondence indicate a Henry Ridge also resided in the area.

Ella Frances (Tallyn) Ridge died May 9, 1929 at age 56. William Ridge died May 7, 1936 at age 80.   3 children

A. Floyd Alvin Ridge:(1891-1977)

Floyd was born August 19,1891 in Woodford County. He was a 1917 graduate of Rockwell City H.S. On December 30, 1918 in Rockwell City Floyd married Helen Means. She was born December 9, 1894.

Helen (Means) Ridge died December 5,1961. Floyd Alvin Ridge died June 31, 1977. (Note: There is evidence indicating Floyd and Helen made their home near Worthington, Minnesota). 2 children

1. Donald Ridge: Donald was born July 15,1920 in Rockwell City (Calhoun Co.), Iowa. On December 28, 1941, in Rockwell City, Donald married Leona Anderson.   Their 2 children were born in Rockwell City. The family makes their home near Worthington, Minnesota.

      a.Gerry Ridge: B. January 2, 1942

      b.Nancy Ridge: B. January 9, 1946

2. William Russell Ridge:[2] Russell was born September 22,1922 in Rockwell City, Iowa.   His wife, Arlene, was born March 2, 1926 in Southland, Minnesota. Their four children were born in Worthington, Minn.

      a.Vickie Sue Ridge: B. July 1,1948

      b.Steven Michael Ridge: B. July 28, 1956

      c. Debra Ann Ridge: B. November 3, 1958

      d. Robert Russell Ridge: B. September 7, 1961

B. Elsie Viola Ridge: (1894-   )

Elsie, the daughter of William and Ella (Tallyn) Ridge, was born July 16, 1894 in Minonk (Woodford Co.),Illinois. On January 21, 1920

---

1 Ridge is an old family name long associated with the villages of
   Stoke Rivers and Loxhore of N. Devon, England. Several families of
   this name settled (1850's) in Woodford and Peoria Counties of Ill.
2 In 1962 Russell Ridge remarried (2nd) No children by this marriage.

Elsie married Frank I. Rose. Frank was born May 23,1895 in Baxter, Iowa. Elsie and Frank make their home in Rockwell City, Iowa where their three children were born.

      1. <u>Earl D. Rose</u>: Earl was born June 3, 1921. On September 26, 1948 he married Betty Harms. Their 2 children were born in Worthington, Minnesota.

            a.<u>Scott William Rose</u>:   B. October 9, 1951.

            b.<u>Reta   Rose</u>: Reta was born October 25, 1955. She is a nurse.

      2. <u>Lynn B. Rose</u>: Lynn was born in Rockwell City, Iowa, May 8, 1923. On December 28, 1950 he married Doris Baxter. She was born August 18,1926 in Lytton, Iowa. Their three children were born in Rockwell City (Calhoun Co.), Iowa.

          a. <u>Kathy Lynn Rose</u>:   B. March 25, 1957

          b.<u>Lori Lee Rose</u>:   B. July 11, 1959

          c.<u>Julie Jo Rose</u>:   B. June 23, 1963

      3. <u>Merle William Rose</u>:   Merle was born March 28, 1926. On December 5, 1948 he married Ardella Martz. Ardella, a nurse, was born October 30,1926. Two children were born to the marriage and both are teachers.

          a.   <u>Linda Kay Rose</u>:   B.July 16, 1950

          b.   <u>Marsha Ann Rose</u>:   B.November 23,1953

C. <u>Ivan Edward Ridge</u>: (1897-   )

     Ivan, the son of William and Ella (Tallyn) Ridge,was born May 13, 1897 in Minonk (Woodford Co.),Illinois. On December 11, 1936 he married Evelyn Kerr. She was born March 3,1904 in Hudson, Iowa. They have made their home at Palmetto near St. Petersburg, Florida.. No Children

              ****
               Notes of Genealogical
                  Interest

  The author is not certain of the orgin of the data underlying this section on the Ridge Family. He has not been successful in contacting a descendant of this family unit. It is important to note that both <u>Elsie (Ridge)Rose</u> and <u>Ivan E. Ridge</u> may belong on the list of most senior Tallyn descendants (See Dedication page).

                ****

V. Lizzie Eva Tallyn: 1864-1953)

Lizzie, the daughter of Joseph and Sarah A. (Daniel)Tallyn, was born near Benson of Woodford County, Illinois, February 12,1864. She grew up in the county and obtained her education in the schools of the county. On February 24,1886 in Minonk, Illinois Lizzie married Charles Stewart Kindig. Charles, the son of Henry Harrison and Sarah Elizabeth (Spitzer) Kindig, was born August 16, 1862 in Augusta County, Virginia. (See Kindig Family in Appendix)

They first made their home in Minonk, Illinois. In 1893 Charles made a trip to Gage County, Nebraska for the purpose of acquiring land. His decision to buy and settle there may have been influenced by the fact his cousin Mary Ann Kindig (1862-1931) and husband Bazalee McCue and family of Benson,Illinois had settled in the county around 1861. Gracele (Kindig) McPherson notes Charles, her grandfather, slected the site because of its relationship to schools and a Brethren Church. Charles deemed both necessary for his children to be of service to the community and humanity.

Charles returned to Illinois and acquired a large rail car to transport the family, their belongings and livestock. They set out for Nebraska by rail February 25, 1893. They settled near Virginia of Gage Co. They affiliated with the Church of the Brethren. Gracele (Kindig)McPherson indicates Joseph and Sarah Daniel were much distressed to learn Lizzie, their Baptist raised daughter,had joined the Brethren Church.[1]

Charles S. Kindig died November 14,1894 at the young age of 32. Lizzie continued to make her home on the farm. She overcame many problems being widowed at such a young age. It is to her credit that their children all obtained an excellent education.

Lizzie Eva (Tallyn) Kindig lived out her life on the farm. She died July 25, 1953 Beatrice (Gage Co.), Nebraska. Charles and Lizzie are buried South Beatrice Church of the Brethren Cemetery, Homeville (Gage Co.), Nebraska.   3 children

A. Ira Nelson Kindig: (1887-1979)

Ira was born January 29,1887 Minonk (Woodford Co.),Illinois. At age six he traveled by train with his parents to Gage Co., Nebraska. Ira was a graduate of the School of Agriculture University of Nebraska (at Lincoln), a farmer and lay preacher. He enjoyed a life-long interest in family history and genealogy.

In August of 1916 in Falls City, Nebraska Ira married Annie Edith Peck. She was the daughter of George W. (1842-1906) and Sarah (Maust) Peck (1841-1938). Annie was born May 3,1844 Falls City (Richardson Co.), Nebraska. Ira and Annie made their home near Homeville, Nebraska. They called their home,Glenwood Farm.

Annie Edith (Peck) Kindig died February 28,1949,Beatrice, Neb. Ira lived out his life in Nebraska. Ira Nelson Kindig died June 15,1979 at age 92 ,Lincoln Neb. Ira and Annie are buried Brethren Cemetery Homeville, Nebraska. Their two children were born at Glenwood Farm near Homeville.

---

1 Charles grandfather, Martin Kindig, was also a member of the Brethren Church.

1. Sarah Arlene Kindig:

   Arlene was born June 17, 1917. She is a graduate of the Business
College of the University of Nebraska. She has worked as a teacher and
secretary to the Supt. of Schools Beatrice, Neb. On July 18,1944, at
the Church of the Brethren (Lincoln, Neb.), Arlene married Junior Earl
Rulla. He is the son of Earl and Nellie (Spence) Rulla. Tech. Sgt. Rulla
served during World War II. He was born July 17,1920, Beatrice, Neb.
Arlene and Earl make their home near Beatrice, Nebraska. 2 children

   a. Irapaul Rulla: Irapaul was born April 9,1945, Beatrice, Neb.
He is a graduate of Beatrice H.S. and is presently in sales. In Beatrice
he married Linda Schmale. Linda, the daughter of Elmer Johnathan Henry
and Alena Elizabeth (Webber) Schmale, was born July 13,1948 in Beatrice.
4 children

   1. Sheila Rulla: B. June 21, 1964 Beatrice, Neb.

   2. Sarah Rulla: B. Oct. 28, 1967 Russellville,Ark.

   3. Debbie Rulla: B. June 17, 1970 Beatrice, Neb.

   4. Terry Rulla:(adopted) Nov.   20, 1967 Omaha, Neb.

   b. Lee Ann Rulla: Lee Ann was born December 31, 1960
Beatrice, Nebraska. She is a graduate of Beatrice H.S. and a student
at North East Missouri College.
                          ******

2. Grace L.E. Kindig:

   Gracele, as she is known, was born October 13,1919 at Glenwood Farm. She notes her initial L.E. stands for Lizzie Eva . Gracele
has a B.S. Degree from Nebraska Wesleyan University (Lincoln, Neb.).
She is a registered nurse (RN) and a graduate of Bryan Memorial
Hospital at Lincoln.
   On September 20, 1942 at South Beatrice Church of the Brethren,
Gracele married Chester George McPherson. He is the son of Samuel Clay
and Minnie Augusta Bertha (Petz) McPherson. Chester was born May 20,
1920 near Adams (Gage Co.), Neb. He is a graduate of the University
of Nebraska (B.S. Degree). He is a teacher and also sells insurance.
Gracele and Chester make their home in Lincoln, Nebraska. 3 Children

   a. Samuel Nelson McPherson: Samuel was born September 20,
1945 Mennonite Hospital Beatrice, Neb. He has a B.S. Degree and a M.S.
Degree from the U. of Nebraska. He is in personel   work.
   On August 5, 1967 Samuel married Mary Louise Heckman. She is the
daughter of Leland L. and Lucille (McDermott) Heckman. Mary was born
September 29, 1945.   2 Children

   1. Heather Amy McPherson: B.Feb. 6,1975 Omaha, Neb.

   2. Lance Scott McPherson: B.Apr. 27, 1978 Oklahoma City,
                             Oklahoma

b. <u>Melodee Ann McPherson</u>:   Melodee was born March 27, 1948
Holdrege (Phelps Co.), Nebraska. She is a graduate (B.S. Degree) of
University of Nebraska. She is a teacher in the State College System
of Nebraska.
   On June 6, 1969, at Jackson Hole, Wyoming, Melodee married David
Morrison Landis. He is the son of Frank and Ruth Mary (Jennings)
Landis. He was born in Lincoln, Nebraska June 10,1948. 2 Children

     1. <u>Mathew David Landis</u>: B. Jan. 27,1970 Lincoln, Nebraska

     2. <u>Melissa Noelle Landis</u>:   March 7, 1973   "   "

   c. <u>Carol Lee McPherson</u>: Carol was born October 31,1951 Holdrege, Neb.
She attended the University of Nebraska. She presently works for the State
Patrol Dept. On June 5, 1971 at Christ United Methodist Church (Lincoln,
Neb.) Carol married Clay Ervin Tucker. Clay was born October 14,1950
and is the son of Ervin Eugene and Bonnie Jean (Schlueter)Tucker.
1 Child
     1. <u>Zachary Ervin Tucker</u>: B. Feb. 19,1979   Lincoln, Nebraska

****

B. <u>Ethel Leta Kindig</u>: (1888-_____)

   Ethel, the daughter of Charles S. and Lizzie Eva (Tallyn)Kindig,
was born July 25,1888, Minonk (Woodford Co.),Illinois. As a youngster
of 5 she traveled with her parents, by train, from Illinois to Gage
County, Nebraska. Ethel and her brothers Sidney and Ira attended Sher-
man School,a one room country school about $\frac{1}{4}$ mile from their home.
Ethel is a graduate of Blue Springs H.S. She is a 1910 graduate of
the School of Agriculture of the University of Nebraska. The commencement
program indicates she was Vice-President of the class.
   At the University,Ethel met Otto H. Liebers (a 1913 graduate).
He and Ira N. Kindig were good friends. On September 3, 1913, Ethel
married Otto Hugo Liebers. He was one of nine children born to August
Christian and Anna (Koehler) Liebers. He was born near Minden (Kearney
Co.), Nebraska, June 25,1887. In 1951 Otto was elected to the Nebraska
State Senate (18th Dist.). He was a national leader of the Guernsey
cattle business and manager of the Nebraska Dairy Development Society.
He was the 1961 Nebraska Hall of Agricultural Achievement Honoree.
Throughout his long and distinguished years of public service Otto was
accompanied by Ethel who shared in the honors, activies and was a
gracious hostess. She was active in the Legislative Ladies League,
Women's Club and the Second Presbyterian Church.
   Otto Hugo Liebers died October 25,1968. He is buried Lincoln Memorial Park Cemetery Lincoln, Nebraska. Ethel Leta (Kindig) Liebers
recently celebrated her 91st. birthday. She makes her home in Lincoln,
Nebraska. 3 Children

80

1. <u>Lawrence Edgar Liebers</u>: Lawrence was born June 14,1914 Beatrice, Nebraska. He is a 1933 graduate of Lincoln H.S. and a 1937 graduate (B.S. Degree) of University of Nebraska. Lawrence was co-owner of Skyline Farms Co. and operated Skyline Dairy and Stores in Lincoln. He is noted for his registered Guernsy herd. His many business interests include Holly Homes, Inc., banking, insurance and flying. He has served on the boards of several church, civic and commercial groups and organizations.

On June 27, 1936, in Casper, Wyoming, Lawrence married Margaret M. Lewin. She is the daughter of Richard Snell and Ethel (Bears) Lewin. Margaret was born August 21,1914 Lead, South Dakota. 2 Children

A. <u>Margaret Ruth Liebers</u>: Margaret was born September 22,1939 Lincoln (Lancaster Co.),Nebraska. She married (first) David Stepan. (No Children) In 1962 Margaret married (2nd.) James Sheldon.(This marriage was also dissolved by divorce) 3 Children

    1. <u>Mike Sheldon</u>:

    2. <u>Jennifer Sheldon</u>:

    3. <u>Elizabeth Sheldon</u>:

B. <u>Kay Marie Liebers</u>: Kay was born in Lincoln, Nebraska,August 20,1941. At Lincoln, on August 15,1964, Kay married Raymond C. Hesse. 3 Children

    1.<u>Robert Arthur Hesse</u>: Robert was born January 26,1968, Shaw Air Force Base, South Carolina.

    2. <u>Christopher Lawrence Hesse</u>: Chris was born August 19,1970, Shaw Air Force Base, South Carolina.

    3. <u>Jonathan Anrdew Hesse</u>: Jonathan was born June 6, 1973, Lincoln, Nebraska.

Raymond C. Hesse died November 20, 1977, Lincoln, Nebraska. He is buried Memorial Park Cemetery (Lincoln, Nebraska).

****

2. <u>Harry Dean Liebers</u>: Harry was born December 6, 1916, Beatrice (Gage Co.),Nebraska. He grew up in Lincoln. He was a graduate of Lincoln H.S. He was in 4H and showed his registered Guernsy heifer calf at the Nebraska State Fair.

Harry entered the University of Nebraska in 1935. He was a Captain in the R.O.T.C. He had a strong interest in military matters. Harry and his brother, Lawrence, started the Skyline Dairy from two heifers.

On August 5, 1936 at Lincoln, Nebraska, Harry married Eleanor Case. She was born August 15,1919. Harry Dean Liebers died(of Hodgkins disease) October of 1937. He is buried Lincoln Memorial Park Gardens (Lincoln, Neb.). 1 child

A. **Geraldine Liebers:** Geraldine was born May 24,1937, Lincoln, Nebraska. At Siloam Springs, Arkansas, she married (Aug. 25,1956) Thomas Ferris. 2 Children

    1. **Thomas Ferris:**   B. November 15, 1959

    2. **Mark Dean Ferris:**   B. April 9,1963, Dallas, Texas

****

3. **Ruth Ethel Liebers:**   Ruth was born July 9,1918, Denver, Colorado. Ruth was a 1937 graduate of Lincoln H.S. (Lincoln, Neb.). She attended the U. of Nebraska (1 yr.). She subsequently worked in Washington, D.C.. She was a member of the Legislative Ladies League. She acted as her father's secretary during his term as State Senator.

In Washington,D.C., Ruth married (April 17, 1942) Robert Cummings Ellis.Together they founded Prairie Bowman in Lincoln. Ruth was active in state archery events and meets. Ruth Ethel (Liebers) Ellis died in April of 1966, Lincoln, Neb. She is buried Lincoln Memorial Park Cemetery.

****

This concludes the family and descendants of Ethel L.(Kindig) and Otto E. Liebers. The author is indebted to Mrs. Lawrence (Margaret) Liebers for making her notes on the family available for use in this document.

****

C.Albert Sidney Kindig: (1890-1974)

      Sidney was born near Minonk (Woodford Co.),Illinois, October 27, 1890. In 1893 at the age of three he traveled with his parents, by train, from Illinois to Gage County, Nebraska. He attended Sherman Grade School, a one room county school near his home. (Virginia, Nebraska). Sidney is a 1912 graduate of the School of Agriculture, University of Nebraska. Colonel Kindig was a staff officer in command of the 1st Regiment of the Nebraska School of Agriculture Cadets.

    At Kansas City School of Law he obtained a degree and subsequently practiced as an attorney in Oakland, Calif. On June 9, 1927 at Beatrice (Gage Co.), Nebraska, Sidney married Letha May Davis. Letha is the daughter of William Henry and Edith May (VanDuyn) Davis. She was born in Wilbur, Nebraska.

    Letha and Sidney made a trip to North Devon, England some years ago. During their visit they made inquires concerning "Aunt" Fanny Daniel, the sister of Sarah A. (Daniel) Tallyn, Sidney's grandmother. "Aunt Fanny" lived to be 93 or 94.   They were unable to locate her. They found the Devon countryside most appealing.

    Albert Sidney Kindig died October 16,1974, Oakland, California, just short of his 84th birthday. He is buried Chapel of the Chimes Cemetery of Oakland. Letha makes her home at Walnut Creek, California.
2 Children

      1. **Marilyn May Kindig:**   Marilyn was born August 21,1930, Berkeley (Alameda Co.), California. On June 15,1950, Marilyn married James William

82

McCartney. Marilyn, a former teacher with the Richmond School District (Richmond, Calif.), is now in the Administration Dept.   3 children

   A. Donald Alan McCartney: Donald was born May 27, 1951 in Berkeley (Alameda Co.),California.

   B. Joan Marie McCartney: Marie was born in Oakland, Calif., March 7, 1953.

   C. James Richard McCartney: James was born November 28,1955 in Oakland, California.

   2. Jeanne Loree Kindig: Jeanne was born in Berkeley (Alameda Co.), California, June 25, 1933. On August 25, 1956 she married a Mr. Riddle. (Now divorced). She is a legal secretary (Lafayette, Calif.).
3 Children

   A. Andrea Lee Riddle: Andrea was born in San Francisco, Calif., September 16,1963.

   B. Mark Aric Riddle: Mark was born January 15, 1966 at Mt. View (Santa Clara Co.), California. He died February 4, 1969.

   C. Dianne Jill Riddle: Dianne was born September 12,1970, Santa Clara (Santa Clara Co.), California

****

This concludes the family and descendants of Sidney and Letha (Davis) Kindig. The author is indebted to Letha M. Kindig for making her notes on the family available for use in this document.

****

Some Notes of Genealogical Interest

Lizzie Eva Tallyn married Charles S. Kindig. Her sister, Alice Augusta Tallyn married Theodore H. Kindig. Charles and Theodore were brothers. The children of each marriage were "double" first cousins.

Some Early Office Holders of Woodford Co.,Illinois

1856	Benj. W. Kindig	Coroner
1843-1845	Benj. W. Kindig	Surveyor
____	W.H. Kindig	Assessor (Green Twp.)

Of Historical Interest

1963 Year Book:Church of the Brethren, page 168

"Ira Kindig   R.D. Homesville, Nebraska "

******

VI. Sarah Irene Tallyn: (1866-1923)

Irene, the daughter of Joseph and Sarah A. (Daniel) Tallyn, was born June 8, 1866 near Benson of Woodford County, Illinois. She grew up and obtained her education in the public schools of the county.

In Woodford County Irene married Herschel James Lee.* He was born in Benson, Illinois November 30, 1862. He was one of seven children born to Thomas and Grace (Huxtable) Lee. (See Lee and Huxtable families in Appendix for additional data) Irene and Herschel first made their home in Woodford County. The 1900 US Census for the County (Green Twp.) lists the family as follows:

****

Lee, Herschel	B. Nov. 1862	age 37	Married 5yrs Farmer B. Ill.
(w) Irene	B. June 1866	33	"
(d) Jennie E.	B. Jan. 1896	4 at home	"
(s) Albert W.	B. Nov. 1899	6 months	"

****

In 1903 the family removed to Garden City (Cass Co.), Missouri. They resided about three miles northeast of the city. They made their home there except for two years (1915-1917) when they resided in Texas. The move to Texas was made for Irene's health. She appears to have had respiratory difficulties.

Sarah Irene (Tallyn) Lee died at home following an attack of pneumonia, March 14, 1923 at age 56. On August 23, 1931 Herschel married (2nd) Ella B. Leadbetter Anderson (1873-1955). No children were born to this marriage. Herschel James Lee died (influenza) June 26, 1942. Irene and Herschel are buried Garden City Cemetery of Garden City, Missouri.
3 Children

*****

1. Jennie Ethel Lee: (1896-1974)

Jennie was born January 6, 1896 in Woodford County, Ill. She was seven when her parents left Benson, Illinois to settle near Garden City, Missouri. She attended Schuyler School. She was a 1917 graduate of Garden City H.S. She attended school at Warrensburg and Springfield Teachers College. She taught elementary school at Eldon, Missouri off and on until 1949.

On April 30, 1924 Jennie married William Bryan Vaughan. William, the son of Charles and Cora (Harrison) Vaughan, was born near Eldon, Missouri May 14, 1898. He was a farmer and a fireman for the Rock Island Railroad.

William B. Vaughan died September 16, 1970. Jennie Ethel (Lee) Vaughan died November 11, 1974. Both are buried Garden City Cemetery, Garden City, Missouri.   1 Child

A. Ethlee Irene Vaughan: Ethlee was born August 26, 1925, Eldon, Missouri. On February 14, 1950 she married Homer Dean Hatfield. She was a member of the Garden City Baptist Church and a graduate of Garden City H.S. She was active in 4H work. Ethlee Irene (Vaughan) Hatfield died July 30, 1974 at age 48. Two children were born to the marriage.

---

* Irene and Herschel were married January 1, 1895 in Woodford Co., Ill.

1. <u>Carl Dean Hatfield</u>:   Carl, a mechanic, was born August 25,1950. On June 6, 1975 he married Peggy Ann Brock. She was born Dec. 9, 1956. 1 Child

        a. <u>Kayce Irene Hatfield</u>: B. June 30, 1977

2. <u>Betty Mae Hatfield</u>:   Betty, a teacher, was born Feb. 5, 1955. On November 3, 1979 she married Alden Guy Brown.

****

2. <u>Albert William Lee</u>: (1899   )

Albert was born on the family farm near Benson (Woodford Co.), Illinois November 12,1899. He is a former high school teacher, principal and Superintendent of Schools. He also did some farming in his youth. Albert, a single man, is retired and makes his home in Harrisonville, Missouri. Albert William Lee is one of the senior members of Tallyn descendants.

****

3. <u>Sheldena Irene Lee</u>: (1908   )

Sheldena was born February 18, 1908 Garden City, Missouri. On September 24, 1930, in Garden City (Cass Co.),Missouri, Sheldena married John William Litle. John was born September 28, 1906, Morrewville, Kansas. He was the son of Steward Henry and Hannah Helena (Schaich) Litle. John was a graduate of Baldwin City H.S. He was a graduate (B.S. Degree) of Baker University (Baldwin City, Kansas).
    In 1935 John and Sheldena bought a farm near Garden City. In 1964 they sold the farm and moved to Harrisonville, Missouri where John was a bookkeeper with Schrock and Yoder Implement Co.
    John William Litle died April 10, 1968(at age 61) at Clinton, Missouri. He is buried Garden City Cemetery of Garden City, Missouri. Sheldena continues to make her home in Harrisonville, Mo. Her interests include genealogy and she is a major biographer for the family and descendants of Sarah Irene (Tallyn) and Herschel James Lee. This work draws heavily upon her efforts, notes and records.
    Three children were born to the marriage of Sheldena and John Litle. They are born in Garden City, Mo.

    A. <u>John Henry Litle</u>:   John was born May 24,1932. He is a 1950 graduate of Garden City H.S. Sgt. John Litle,an army veteran, served in Korea (1953-54). He was awarded the Commendation Ribbon for distinguished service with the 143rd Field Artillery Battalion 40th Infantry Division.
    On August 19, 1956 John married Blanche Nadine Bates. She is the daughter of Mr. and Mrs. Karl Bates. Blanche, a teacher, was born August 15, 1936. 4 Children

85

1. Philip David Litle: B. February 3,1960

2. Mark Alan Litle: B. April 4, 1962

3. Stephen Duane Litle: B. May 12, 1963

4. Suzanne Jeanette Litle: B. August 16, 1967

****

B. Richard Lee Litle: Richard was born August 13,1933. He
is a 1951 graduate of Garden City High School. On August 15,1961
Richard married Nanetta Nell Milburn. Nanetta was born July 20, 1932.
In 1968 Richard and Nanetta made their home in Independence, Missouri.
Both are trained as teachers.   2 Children

1. Lee Ann Litle: B. September 21, 1962

2. Lisa Kay Litle: B. August 3, 1963

****

C. Margaret Ann Litle: Margaret was born August 29, 1936.
She is a 1954 graduate of Garden City H.S. and a 1955 graduate of
Kansas City Business College. She worked for Kansas City Power and
Light Co.
On April 7, 1957 at Garden City Baptist Church Margaret married Glen
Dale Riffle. He is the son of Mr. and Mrs. Glen Riffle of Holden,
Missouri. Glen was born May 19,1934. He is a veteran (US Marine Corp).
At the time of marriage Glen worked for the Goldblatt Tool Co. They
made their home in Kansas, City, Missouri.   3 Children

1. Janet Denise Riffle: Janet, a nurse, was born June
27, 1958.

2. Paul Michael Riffle: B. October 20, 1960

3. Lora Ann Riffle: B. October 15, 1964

****
Of Historical Interest

Herschel James Lee traveled to Kansas, Colorado and Nebraska in
1887 to prove upon claims there two of which he held until the
time of his death. He returned to Illinois in 1893.

VII. <u>Newton Elmore Tallyn: 1868-1868)</u>

Newton Elmore was the seventh of ten children born to Joseph and Sarah A. (Daniel) Tallyn. He was born near Benson(Woodford Co.), Ill., September 10, 1868. He died shortly after on September 26, 1868. His mother, Sarah, wrote the following memorium marking the event. It was spoken by Arthur H. Tallyn (age 11) at the memorial services.

In Rememberance of Little Newton

1. Do your remember little school mates,
   Not so very long ago,
   That we had an angel brother.
   Whom they laid in yonder tomb?

2. Some may think me very silly,
   Thus to talk of one so small,
   But it was our darling baby,
   And we loved him one and all.

3. Tho its life was as a vapour,
   And it vanished quick away,
   It was the will of God, who gave it,
   To take our little one away

4. And we dare not murmer at it,
   When we know our little boy,
   Has gone to live with holy angels,
   In that world of peace and joy.

5. Other children here I know,
   Have little loved ones gone,
   Taken by death's cold hand away,
   They are in that happy home.

6. Where we are told the Blessed Saviour,
   When he went from earth away,
   'Twas to prepare a heavenly mansion,
   For those who on Him do rely.

7. May we ever, little school mates,
   Love and serve the Saviour kind,
   Who did leave the realms of glory,
   And for you and me He died.

8. If we trust and love and serve Him
   While in this world we stay,
   We shall join those darling loved ones,
   And live with them in endless day.

****

Note: The original version of the poem is in the handwriting of Sarah Tallyn. A later version was printed to mark the death of a small female child. In this later edition the word "girl" appears in place of <u>boy</u> in the original version, etc.

VIII. Newton Oscar Tallyn: (1869-1949)

Newton, the son of Joseph and Sarah A. (Daniel) Tallyn, was born August 21, 1869 near Benson of Woodford County, Illinois. Newton appears on the 1870 and 1880 US Census years for the County under the household of his father as : Newton age 11 months and Newton age 10, respectively.

In Benson Newton married (February 26, 1896) Mary Anna Eckhart. Mary was born June 19, 1872 Benson, Illinois. She was one of several children born to Adam and Anna (Roth) Eckhart. Her father was born in 1840 in Cincinnati, Ohio and her mother 1849 in Spring Bay, Illinois.[1] Her siblings included Jacob, Henry, Emma and Amelia Eckhard.

Newton was a farmer of Woodford County. The 1900 US Census for the County shows the family residing in Clayton Twp. as follows:

Tallyn, N.O.	B. Aug. 1869 age 30	married 4yrs	Farmer	B. Illinois
(w) Mary	B. June 1873	26	Keeping house	Illinois
(s) Everett	B. May 1897	3	at home	Illinois

****

Anna Mary (Eckhart) Tallyn died June 21, 1933 (age 61), Bloomington, Illinois. Newton Oscar Tallyn died November 7, 1949 at age 80, Minonk, Illinois. Both are buried Clayton Cemetery near Benson (Woodford Co.), Illinois.   4 children

1. Everett Arthur Tallyn: (1897-1925)

Everett was born May 18, 1897 near Benson (Woodford Co.), Illinois. He died (June 21, 1925) at age 28, as a result of a drowning which took place at Miller Park Bloomington, Illinois. Everett is buried Clayton Cemetery of Benson (Woodford Co.), Illinois.

2. Arden Newton Tallyn: (1902-1968)

Arden was born January 24, 1902, Benson, Illinois. On August 11, 1933, in Minonk (Woodford Co.), Illinois, Arden married Florence Uphoff. She was born December 14, 1910 in Minonk. She is the daughter of Otto J. and Anna (Folkers) Uphoff. Florence is a descendant of two (Uphoff&Folkers) pioneer families of Woodford County, Illinois.

The family made their home near Benson where Arden farmed most of his life. He was a member of Woodford County Farm Bureau. Arden Newton Tallyn died December 9, 1968 (Eureka Hospital) Woodford Co., Illinois. He is buried Clayton Township Cemetery near Benson, Ill.   3 children

a. <u>Arnold Tallyn:</u> Arnold was born October 18, 1934, Streator (LaSalle Co.), Illinois. On December 28, 1977 he married Victoria Schirer. Victoria, the daughter Emerald and Doris (Williams) Schirer, was born in Streator, Illinois.   1 child

1. <u>Arnold Tallyn (Jr.):</u> B. August 18, __?__ Streator, Ill.

---

[1] 1880 US Census data indicates Adam's father was born in the Duchy of Hesse, (Germany).

b. <u>Arlene Tallyn</u>:

       Arlene was born August 10, 1936 ,Streator, Illinois. At
St. Paul Luthern Church (Benson, Ill.) she married (Jan. 9,1960)
Donald Wolf. Donald was born in Benson, March 27, 1934. He is the
son of Joseph and Pearl (Uphoff) Wolf. Arlene works for Benson Farmers
Co-Op Grain Association. The family makes its home in Benson, Ill.
Their four children were born in Pontiac (Livingston Co.), Illinois.

     1. <u>Gary L. Wolf</u>:   B. April 3, 1964

     2. <u>Stacy J. Wolf</u>:   B. July 10, 1969

     3. <u>Karla K. Wolf</u>:   B. October 30, 1972

     4. <u>Marla R. Wolf</u>:   B. October 30, 1972

c. <u>Anne Tallyn</u>:

       Anne, the daughter of Arden Newton and Florence(Uphoff)
Tallyn, was born July 29,1940, Pontiac (Livingston Co.),Illinois.
On September 1, 1962, at St John Catholic Church of Benson, Anne
married James A. Kapraum. James was born March 28, 1938, Streator, Ill.
He is the son of Frank and Louise (Meyers) Kapraum. 6 Children

     1.<u>Michael Kapraum</u>:   B. June 20, 1963 Ft. Huachuca, Arizona

     2.<u>Daniel Kapraum</u>:   B. Apr. 28, 1964 Peoria (Peoria Co.),Ill.

     3.<u>Charles Kapraum</u>:   B. Dec. 15, 1966   "   "   "

     4.<u>Benjamin Kapraum</u>: B. Jan. 30,1969   "   "   "

     5.<u>Bruce Kapraum</u>:   B. Aug. 11,1972   "   "   "

     6.<u>Kathleen Kapraum</u>: B. June 6,1976   "   "   "

****

3. <u>Lloyd Emmett Tallyn</u>: (1903   )

      Lloyd, the son of Newton O. and Mary (Eckhart) Tallyn, was born
October 12, 1903 near Benson (Woodford Co.),Illinois. In Kankakee, Ill.,
Lloyd married (August 21,1929) Lola G. Pester (b. Jan. 5,1900). She was
born in Manhattan, Illinois. She is the daughter of George and Mary
Graves Pester. 2 children

     1. <u>David O. Tallyn</u>: B. Jan.18,1935 Columbus (Franklin Co.),Ohio
                            D. Jan.21,1935   "   "   "

     2. <u>Lee I. Tallyn</u>:   B. Feb.29,1936 Columbus (Franklin Co.),Ohio
                           D. Sept.11,1962. Germany
                           Buried: Arlington National Cemetery

****

4. <u>Lela Opal Tallyn</u>: (1912-1963)

　　Lela, the daughter of Newton O. and Mary (Eckhart) Tallyn, was born June 21,1912 (rural route) Benson (Woodford Co.), Illinois. In Roanoke, Illinois at the Roanoke Methodist Parsonage, Lela married (Dec. 26,1936) Henry Seifka deFreese. Henry, the son of Reinke and Carrie (Peters) de Freese, was born March 12,1911 near Benson, Illinois. It is of genealogical interest to note that several individuals of the deFreese family name settled in Woodford County, Illinois around 1867. Various US census records for the county indicate they came to the US from Hanover, Germany.

　　Lela Opal (Tallyn)deFreese died, June 5, 1963, about two weeks prior to her 51st birthday. She is buried Clayton Township Cemetery near Benson. Henry, a farmer, continues to make his home in Woodford County. (Note: He married (2nd) Pauline (Behrends) Backer: No Children)

　　Three children were born to the marriage of Lela and Henry.

　　A. <u>Larry Franklin deFreese</u>: Larry was born July 21,1938,Streator (LaSalle Co.),Illinois. In Toluca, Illinois, Larry married (Feb.6,1965) Judy Kay Madole. Judy was born in Freeport, Illinois, June 20, 1946. She is the daughter of James and Yvonne (Frederick) Madole.

　　Larry is a farmer and farm equipment dealer and parts manager.He and Judy make their home near Benson (Rural Route), Illinois.
2 Children

　　　　1. <u>Brian Scott deFreese</u>: B. Feb. 17,1965 Streator LaSalle Co., Illinois.

　　　　2. <u>Barry Dale deFreese</u>: B. March 15, 1970 Streator, Illinois.

　　　　　　　　　*****

　　B. <u>Richard Henry deFreese</u>: Richard was born Pontiac, Illinois, May 1, 1940.He is a mechanicfor Catepillar Tractor Co. In Benson, Illinois Richard married(July 27,1968) Arlene May. She is the daughter of Harry and Lorene (Punke) May. Arlene was born February 27, 1942, Bloomington, Illinois.   3 Children

　　　　1. <u>Debra Mae deFreese</u>: B. May 2,1969 Streator (LaSalle Co.),Ill.

　　　　2. <u>Denise June deFreese</u>:B. June 23, 1971 "   "   "

　　　　3. <u>David Richard deFreese</u>: B.Aug. 10,1972 Normal (McLean Co.),Ill.

　　　　　　　　　******

　　C. <u>Dale William deFreese</u>: Dale was born March 21, 1946, Pontiac, Ill. On July 25, 1970 at Benson, Ill. , Dale married Linda Klyce. She is the daughter of Charles and Dorothy (Lonon) Klyce. She was born Jan. 4, 1950, Friendship, Tennessee. Dale works for Catepillar Tractor Co. Their <u>2</u> children were born in Peoria (Peoria Co.), Illinois.

　　　　1.<u>Ryan Dale deFreese</u>:   B.April 23, 1975

　　　　2.<u>Rachel Lynne deFreese</u>: B. March 23, 1977.

The author is indebted to Mrs. Donald Wolf (Arlene Tallyn) who made her notes on the family of Newton O. and Mary (Eckhart) Tallyn available for use in this document.

IX. Alice Augusta Tallyn: (1872-1951)

Alice, the daughter of Joseph and Sarah A. (Daniel) Tallyn, was born on the family farm near Benson August 5, 1872. She grew up in Woodford County, Illinois where she obtained her education. On February 15, 1893 in Woodford County Alice married Theodore Henry Kindig. He was a brother to Charles who married Lizzie Eva Tallyn, a sister to Alice., Theodore was born in Woodford County, October 7, 1867. He was the son of Henry Harrison Kindig (1830-1914) and Sarah Elizabeth Spitzer (1843-1926).(See Kindig Family in Appendix)

The family first made their home in Benson,Illinois where 5 of their 8 children were born. They lived in Rankin, Illinois for about a year prior to moving to New Carlisle, Indiana in 1909. Around 1912 they moved to San Benito, Texas. They lived in North Dakota about two years prior to settling in Petaluma, California in 1919. They raised chickens commercially on a farm near Petaluma.

Alice Augusta (Tallyn) Kindig, died June 7, 1951 just two months prior to her 84th birthday. Theodore Henry Kindig died May 6, 1940. They died in Petaluma and both are buried in Two Rock Cemetery of Petaluma (Sonoma Co.), California   8 Children

1. Lelia May Kindig: (1894-   )

Lelia was born in Benson of Woodford County, Illinois, February 3, 1894. On August 26, 1916 in San Benito, (Cameron Co.), Texas Lelia married Harry G. Thompson.* Lelia and Harry settled in Bakersfield, California where they raised wine grapes.

Harry G.. Thompson died October 26,1975.. He is buried in Bakersfield (Kern Co..), California. Lelia continues to make her home in Bakersfield. 1 Child

A. Mary Alice Thompson: Mary was born May 26, 1917 in Werner (Dunn Co.), North Dakota. In April of 1943 she married Ray Huffman. He was born December 12, 1919. Mary Alice (Thompson) Huffman died July 2, 1954 at age 38, in Bakersfield, Calif.. 2 Children

> 1. Karen Huffman: Karen was born in Bakersfield, .
> June 13, 1944. She married David Spease. He was born
> December 1,1944. 2 Children
>
>> a. Kristen Spease: B..August 18, 1966
>>
>> b. Kevin Spease: B. October 5, 1968
>
> 2. Lelia Huffman: Lelia was born June 15, 1948.
> She was most likely born in Bakersfield, Calif.

---

* Harry G. Thompson was born in Eureka, Calif. He was the son of William and Mary "Mollie" (Stockton) Thompson.

2. <u>Leslie Owen Kindig:</u> (1897-   )

Leslie was born near Benson of Woodford County, Illinois,
February 28, 1897. He obtained his education in the schools of Wood-
ford County and New Carlisle(Joseph Co.), Indiana.
On October 19,1918 in Killdeer, North Dakota Leslie married
Thora Langie. She was born May 5,1897 in Crookston, Minnesota. She
is the daughter of Targie and Bergit (Hagland) Langie. Her parents
were born in Norway.
Leslie, now retired, worked for a Petaluma feed mill. Thora
enjoys sewing as a leisure time activity. Both are members of the
Elim Luthern Church of Petaluma.   1 Child

A. <u>Theodore Alvin Kindig:</u> Theodore was born September 29, 1919
in Killdeer, North Dakota. He married Betty Simonson. (Now Divorced)
3 Children
1. <u>Marsha Kindig:</u> Marsha was born in Petaluma. She married
George Hutchinson. They own and operate a trucking firm
in the San Francisco area. They make their home nearby at
Novato, Calif.   2 Children

a. <u>Erica Lynn Hutchinson:</u> B. 1970 (?) She
was born in San Francisco, Calif..

b. <u>Jessica Ann Hutchinson:</u> B. 1973 (?) She
was born in San Francisco.

2. <u>Keith Theodore Kindig:</u> Keith was born in Petaluma,
Calif. He married Linda Simonson. She was born in Thief
River Falls, Minnesota. Keith is a Title Officer with an
Oakland, California firm.   Keith and Linda make their home
in nearby Union City, Calif. 1 Child

a. <u>Erin Ann Kindig:</u> B. September 29,1979
Union City, California

3. <u>Jack Leslie Kindig:</u> Jack was born in San Francisco,
Calif. Jack and his wife, Terri, make their home in
Hayward, California. He is a bookkeeper for the trucking
firm of his brother-in-law,George Hutchinson. 1 Child

a. <u>Justin Keith Kindig:</u> B. April of 1978
San Francisco, Calif.

****
3. <u>Ruth Alta Kindig:</u>(1900-   )

Ruth was born near Benson of Woodford County, Illinois, Nov. 4,
1900. On May 10, 1930 she married Jim Hamilton. Ruth and Jim make
their home in Petaluma, California. No Children

****

4. <u>Raymond Elmo Kindig</u>: (1903-1969)

Raymond was born near Benson of Woodford County, Illinois, Nov. 1, 1903. On December 9, 1928 Raymond married Angie Garrity. Raymond died February 20, 1969. No Children

****

5. <u>Merton Dwight Kindig</u>: (1906-1979)

Merton was born near Benson (Woodford Co.),Illinois.* In Santa Rosa, California he married (June 4, 1927) Vira Kindig. Vira was born July 12, 1907 in Santa Rosa. She is the daughter of LeRoy and Sally (Diffin) Kindig.(See Kindig Family in Appendix)
    Merton worked for G. P. McNear Co. of Petaluma, Calif. In 1947 the family moved to Bakersfield, California where Merton farmed some 17 years and later worked as a dispatcher for Valley Nitrogen of Bakersfield.
    Merton Dwight Kindig died October 1, 1979 at age 73. He is buried Hillcrest Memorial Park of Bakersfield. Vira continues to make her home at Bakersfield.   2 Children

    A <u>Barbara Joyce Kindig</u>: Barbara was born May 22, 1928 in Petaluma, Calif.. She obtained her elementary education in Petaluma. She graduated from high school in Santa Rosa, Calif..She attended (2yrs) Bakersfield Junior College. Barbara worked for the US Post Office at Bakersfield.
    Barbara Joyce Kindig died May 20, 1978. She is buried Hillcrest Memorial Park of Bakersfield, California. No Descendants

    B. <u>Gail Alyne Kindig</u>: Gail was born November 17, 1934 in Petaluma (Sonoma Co.), California. She is a graduate of Kern County Union H.S. (1952) and a 1956 graduate of Pepperdine University at Los Angeles, California. At Pepperdine she was awarded a B.S. Degree in Business. She was a yell leader at Pepperdine (1955-57). Since graduation Gail has worked as a substitute teacher (elementary level) for the Kern County School District. She worked as a secretarty for Kern County and the Sheriff's Dept.
    On March 26, 1960 Gail married Bill J.Moore. Bill was born in Chandler, Oklahoma, May 12, 1930. He is the son of Poston J. and Minnie Lee (Leonard) Moore. Bill served in the US Navy (1950-54) where he obtained the rank of 2nd Class Machinist Mate. He is a 1975 graduate of Bakersfield Junior College (A.A. Degree in Fire Science). Bill, a fireman, works for the Kern County Fire Dept. The family makes their home at Bakersfield, Calif. 3 Children

        1.<u>Michelle Denise Moore</u>: Michelle was born in Bakersfield (Kern Co.),Callifornia February 21, 1961. She is a student at Abilene Christian College (Abilene, Texas). She is a Physical Education Major.

        2. <u>Marguerite Ann Kindig</u>: Marguerite was born April 19,1963 in Bakersfield, Calif. She is a junior at North High School ..She

_____
*

Merton Dwight Kindig was born March 28, 1906

received   honors in citizenship and is listed in the 1978 and 1979 editions of Who's Who Of American Students.

3. Cherese Sally Moore: Cherese was born in Bakersfield, California July 12, 1972. She is in the second grade at Highland Elementary School of Bakersfield.

****

6. Edith Genevieve Kindig: (1908-   )

Edith was born March 16, 1908 in New Carlisle (Joseph Co.), Indiana. On November 28, 1927 in Petaluma (Sonoma Co.),California Edith married Ralph Roy Pitney. He was born in Inavale (Webster Co.), Nebraska, December 16, 1899. Ralph was the son of Clyde Gilson and Carrie (Reigle) Pitney.
Ralph R. Pitney died May 28, 1977. He is buried at Bakersfield, California. 2 Children

A.   Virginia Lee Pitney: Virginia was born December 2, 1932, Coalinga(Fresno Co.), California. In Bakersfield, California Virginia married (Aug. 29,1953) Philip Scott Nicola. He is the son of Burnett Cooper and Madge Ella (Watkins) Nicola. Philip was born August 25,1932 in South Gate, California. (Virginia and Philip were divorced August 13, 1979) Virginia makes her home in Mission Viejo, Calif. Their 4 children were born in Bakersfield (Kern Co.), California.

1. Claire Darise Nicola: B. June 20, 1958

2. Kathyrn Janise Nicola: B. November 28, 1959

3. Constance Elsie Nicola: B. June 20, 1962

4. Christopher Adam Nicola: B. February 12, 1964

B.   Martin LeRoy Pitney: Martin was born in Los Angeles, California August 7, 1944.. In October of 1966 in Sacramento, California Martin married Michelle Marie Appel. She was born August 5, 1947 in Sacramento. Michelle is the daughter of Leo H. and Marie Appel. 3 children

1. Troy Martin Pitney: B..October 15, 1974

2. Brent Michael Pitney: B..February 1, 1977

3..Mindy Michelle Pitney: B. September 5, 1978

****

7. Vera Alice Kindig: (1910-   )

Vera was born in New Carlisle (Joseph Co.),Indiana March 30, 1910. Vera married John Cook. John died December 31, 1964.

Vera makes her home in Bakersfield, California. 2 Children

        A. Ruth Alice Cook: (1931—1978) Ruth married Elmer
Hill. 1 Child

                1. John Hill: John served in the U.S. Navy. In
August of 1976 he married Pamela. They make their
home in Bakersfield Calif. 1 Child

                      a. Patsy York (foster child)

        B. Linda Mae Cook: Linda married Jerry Oldham. They make
their home in Bakersfield, California.

******

8. Edwin Theodore Kindig: (1914-   )

    Edwin was born October 21,1914 in San Benito (Cameron Co.),
Texas. Around 1916 the family moved to North Dakota and in 1919
they settled in Petaluma California. Edwin grew up in Petaluma
where his father had a chicken farm. He obtained his elementary and
secondary schooling in Petaluma.
    At age 19 Edwin went to work for his sister and brother-in-law,
Lelia and Harry G. Thompson of Bakersfield, Calif. In Bakersfield
at age 21 he married (May 10, 1936) Louise Katherine Luhmann. She
was born April 15, 1915 in Poppenbuttell (near Hamburg),Germany.
Louise is the daughter of Herman Henry and Caroline (Beckmann)
Luhmann.
    In 1942 Edwin started diversified farming(i.e., 98 acres cotton,
grapes &alfalfa) on his own. Since retirement Edwin and Louise
have made their home at Bakersfield and Cayacos, California.
2 children

        A. Donald Edwin Kindig: Donald was born June 27, 1939 in
Bakersfield, Calif. In Bakersfield he married (Sept. 12, 1958) Donna
Mae Armacost. Donna, the daughter of Joe and Ada (Plumley) Armacost,
was born in Bakersfield December 3, 1938. Donald and his brother,
Gerald, farm 620 acres of wine grapes in the Bakersfield area.
2 children

                1. Douglas Craig Kindig: B. December 20, 1960. He works
on the family farm.

                2. Darren Eric Kindig: B. March 1, 1963. Darren attends
high school.

        B. Gerald Lee Kindig: Gerald was born May 22, 1942 in Bakers-
field, Calif. Gerald married (June 17,1961)Betty Lou Mitchell. She
is the daughter of Kenneth and Ruth(Cordell) Mitchell and was born in
Arvin, California, June 14, 1942. In 1979 the 620 acre family farm
produced 6,150 tons of wine grapes. 2 children

                1. Stan Lee Kindig: B.Sept.21, 1963 Bakersfield, Calif.
                2. Robert Martin Kindig: B. June 2,1964   "   "

****

X. Louis Liston Tallyn: (1878-1960)

Louis was the tenth and last child born to Joseph and Sarah A. (Daniel) Tallyn. The bible of Joseph and Sarah lists Louis as follows:

"Lewis Listen Tallyn was born August 5th 1878"

Louis was born on the family farm near Benson of Woodford County, Illinois. He obtained his education in the public schools of the county. He was a 1901 graduate of the University of Illinois. His B.S. of Degree was in Engineering. Louis was Division Engineer for the Lackawanna and Western Railroad Co. Scranton, Pennsylvania.

In 1907 Louis married Edith Mary Adamson. She was the daughter of John Evans Adamson (1859-1918) and Ann Marie Dennis(1862-1916). She was born February 26,1883. The family made their home in Scranton, Pennsylvania and Chatham, New Jersey. Louis was a Civil War enthusiast. He was knowledgeable about battles and Civil War personalities.

Louis Liston Tallyn died in 1960. Their three children were probably born in Scranton (Lackawanna Co.),Pennsylvania.

A. William Henry Tallyn:

William was born August 27, 1908. He was educated in the law. Judge Tallyn served as Refree in Bankruptcy for United States District Court of New Jersey. William married (1st) Margareta Dilner. She was born in 1910. They first made their home in Trenton, New Jersey. 4 Children

1.William Louis Tallyn:	B.1935
2.Robert Douglas Tallyn:	B.1939
3.Peggy Lee Tallyn:	B.1944
4.Dennis A. Tallyn:	B.1949 (Now Deceased)

William and Margareta were divorced in 1958. In 1959 William married (2nd) Dorothy Frick Bryan. She was born in 1916. 1 Child

5.Jean Ann Tallyn:	B. 1959

****

B. Mirian Adamson Tallyn:

Miriam was born October 11, 1911(another source gives the 21st). She married Clement Jacob Koeferl. He was born February 14,1911. The family first made their home near Dover, New Jersey where Clement worked for an explosive plant. In 1950 they moved to Carthage of

96

Jasper County, Missouri. At Carthage Clement worked for Hurcules Powder Co. as Supervisor of the Dynamite Dept. Their six children were probably born in New Jersey.

1. Mary Constance Koeferl: B. April 14,1935

2. Katherine Tallyn Koeferl: B. November 27,1936

3. Clement John Koeferl: B. March 29, 1942

4. Michael Tallyn Koeferl: B. February 1, 1945

5. Margareta Agnes Koeferl: B. July 28, 1948

6. Peter Kevin Koeferl: B. January 24, 1952

****

C. Harriet Ethel Tallyn:

Harriet was born April 17,1918 (another source indicates the 25th). She married Allen James Wiseman. He was born in 1916. They resided in Mendham, New Jersey. Allan was Staff Assistant to the Plant Manager of Westinghouse Elevator Co.   3 Children

1. Jane T. Wiseman: B. May of 1944

2. Suzanne T. Wiseman: B. June 21,1950

3. William T. Wiseman: B. February 8, 1953

******

This section draws heavily from the efforts of DeWitt Tallyn (1891-1960) of Benson, Illinois and Ethel Adamson Sturgis of Portland, Oregon. She is the author of:

John Evans Adamson
Kill-Clifden, Conamara, County Galway, Ireland
Private Printing: 1957

The author is also indebted to Mrs. C.G. McPherson (Gracele Kindig) of Lincoln, Nebraska, for making her notes on the family of Louis and Edith (Adamson) Tallyn available for use in this document.

This concludes the listing of the children and descendants of Joseph and Sarah A. (Daniel) Tallyn

*****

APPENDICES

ALLIED FAMILIES

Some Major Family Lines Associated With the Tallyn Line

By Marriage

****

I   The Fry Family

II   The Ford Family

III   The Lee Family

IV   The Forney Family

V   The Huxtable Family

VI   The Kindig Family

VII   The Daniel and Conibear Families

VIII The Heiken Family

IX   The McCue and Jones Families

****

The Fry Family:

The history of the Fry Family is said to date back to the time of Alfred The Great. Interest in this family stems from the marriages of: Thomas R. Tallyn and Elizabeth Fry, William W. Tallyn and Louisa Fry, and Frederick N. and Emilie (Fry) Tallyn.

1.Thomas Fry and Betsy Snell of Swimbridge:

Thomas Fry was born about 1800 at Swimbridge of the Parish of Swimbridge of North Devon, England. Around 1825 he married Betsy Snell. She was born at Little Torrington of North Devon around 1800. Eight children were born to the marriage.

Elisabeth Fry: was born at Swimbridge in 1826. In Devon she married (1847) Thomas R. Tallyn. In 1847 they sailed for America settling in Peoria Co.,Ill. Seven children were born to the marriage. Their son William W. Tallyn married (about 1878) Louisa Fry, the daughter of Agnes(Lee)and Abraham Fry.

Phoebe Ann Fry: was born Jan. 14,1827 at Swimbridge. In Devon she married (March 14,1850) John Ford.They settled in Peoria Co.,Ill.

George H. Fry: was born about 1828 at Swimbridge. Around 1850 he settled in Peoria Co.,Illinois and later Woodford Co. His wife, Della was born in Ohio about 1838.

Thomas Fry: was born in Swimbridge Dec. 24,1832. In Devon he married (Apr. 20,1858) Christine Symons (Simmons). Kate, the daughter of Robert and Ann (Hartwell) Symons was born in Bratton Fleming July 12,1836. They settled in Peoria Co.,Illinois in 1859.

John (1833), Frederick (1835) Lucy (1840) and Geo. H. Fry,II (1844), are children of Thomas and Betsy (Snell) Fry who appear to have remained in England.

Thomas and Betsy moved to Stoke Rivers around 1842 where Geo. H. Fry, II was born. Thomas died between 1861 and 1871 and Betsy at some point after 1871. *******

2. Abraham Fry and Agnes Lee of Swimbridge and Stoke Rivers:

Abraham, the brother to Thomas Fry, was born in Swimbridge around 1811. Around 1835 he married Agnes Lee (b. 1813:Stoke Rivers), the daughter of Thomas and Mary Lee of Lower Davis of Stoke River Parish. At least nine children were born to the marriage. Two of their children, John and Louisa Fry, are of special interest.

John Fry: John was born about 1837. He married Susanna Lee (b. 1838: Goodleigh of N. Devon), the daughter of William and Susanna (Davie) Lee.(See Thomas and Mary Lee in Appendix.) John and Susanna first made their home at Lower Davis of Stoke Rivers where Polly B. (1864), Emilie L. (1866), Abraham (1868), Elizabeth (1870), and probably John Fry (1873) were born.

The family settled in Woodford County, Illinois in 1873. They were accompanied by John's father (a widower) Abraham Fry, Susanna (Davie) Lee, and Richard Lee (brother-in-law). In America Emilie L. Fry married Frederick Newton Tallyn the son of Anthony and Susanna (Lee) Tallyn.

Louisa Fry: Louisa, the daughter of Abraham and Agnes (Lee) Fry, was born about 1857 in Stoke Rivers. She married William W. Tallyn. He was the son of Thomas R. and Elizabeth (Fry) Tallyn. They made their home in Peoria County, Illinois.

*****

Other children of Abraham and Agnes (Lee) Fry included: Thomas (1839), Elizabeth (1842), Richard (1843) Henry (1846), Mary (1849), Agnes (1851) and Ann Fry (1854).

Agnes (Lee) Fry, the wife of Abraham, died at some point between 1861-1871. Abraham settled in America. He died prior to 1900. He was living at the time of the 1880 US Census which shows him residing under the household of his son-in-law and daughter William W. and Louisa (Fry) Tallyn of Peoria Co., Illinois. His age is given as 69.

****

Some Notes of Interest

1880 U.S. Census Woodford Co., Illinois

Fry, John	age 43	Druggist	Born: England
(w)Susanna	43		"
(d)Polly B.	16		"
(d)Emilie L.	14		England
(s) Aby (Abraham)	12		"
(d) Lizzie L.	10		"
Lee,Susanna	67	(Mother-in-law)	England

****

John Fry was a farmer of 136 acres at Lower Davis of Stoke Rivers. In America he became a druggist. The 1900 U.S. Census for Woodford Co., Illinois, lists John Fry (age 67, druggist) under the household of Frederick Newton Tallyn and his grand-daughter, Emilie (Fry).

***

3.James Fry was born around 1809 at Swimbridge of North Devon. He is very likely a brother to Thomas and Abraham Fry of this sketch. His wife, Ellen, was born about 1812 at nearby Kentisbury. James worked in agriculture and as a butcher. They made their home in Stoke Rivers. Their children included: James (1833), Henry (1836), Thomas (1838), Jessie (1840) and Frederick Fry (1844). It is not certain whether or not any children of this family ever married into the Tallyn Line.

***

It is important to note that birth dates are, for the most part estimated from census and christening records. and may differ by a year or so from the actual year of birth.

APPENDIX II

THE FORD FAMILY [1]

****

John Ford was a brother-in-law to Thomas R. and Elizabeth (Fry) Tallyn. Elizabeth's sister, Pheobe Ann Fry married John Ford. They were married March 4, 1850 and the event is recorded in the book of Barnstaple Marriages Vol. X p. 97 , 2nd quarter, 1851. (Date of recording may not correspond to actual marriage date)

John Ford was born, March 12, 1820 in the Parish of Bishops Tawton Devon, England. He was the son of Samuel and Sarah (Smaldridge) Ford of Bishops Tawton. His grandfather was Samuel Ford. His maternal grandparents were Anthony and Sarah Smaldridge.

Shortly after their marriage in 1850 John and Phoebe sailed for America, landing in New York. They went west by way of Buffalo and Sandusky to Chicago. From Chicago they came by the Illinois and Michigan Canal and by river (Illinois) to Peoria.

They first settled in Kickapoo township and later Section 32 of Radnor township of Peoria County, Illinois. The farm, originally purchased in conjunction with Thomas R. Tallyn, his brother-in-law, was the site where their eight children were raised. Their children included:

1. <u>John William Ford</u>(b. about 1852) : He married Sarah Williams

2. <u>Frederick Francis Ford</u> (b. about 1854): He married Nettie Brown.

3. <u>James Henry Ford</u> (b. about 1856): He married Georgia Forney.

4. <u>Samuel Thomas Ford</u> (b. about 1860): He married Isabel Harris.

5. <u>Charles Robert Ford</u>(b. about 1864): He married Luta Forney.

6. <u>Albert Ford</u> (b. about 1865): He died prior to 1900.

7. <u>Henry Ford</u> (no birth data available): died prior to 1900.

8. <u>Lucyy Amelia Ford</u>(no birth data) :died prior to 1900.

****

Mary Ford: Mary, a sister to John Ford, was born,July 12,1817. She married Philip Corney of Devon, England. Mary and Philip came to America in 1850. They settled in Jubilee township of Peoria Co., Illinois.

---

1 Data for the Ford family excerpted from: <u>Historical Encyclopedia of Peoria County, Illinois</u>, (editor) David McCulloch, Vol. II, p. 801, 1902.
Other sources include the <u>1870</u> and <u>1880 US Census for Peoria Co., Illinois.</u>

APPENDIX III

<u>The Lee Family of Lower Davis</u>
<u>Parish of Stoke Rivers</u>:

Interest in the Lee Family stems from a number of marriages between Lee and Tallyn descendants. Of special interest is the relationship between <u>William</u>,<u>Agnes</u> and <u>Susanna Lee</u> and Tallyn descendants.

***

1. <u>Thomas Lee</u>: Thomas was born in Goodleigh of North Devon about 1780. His wife, Mary, was born about 1782 in Charles of N. Devon. They were married around 1806. They first made their home at Goodleigh where <u>William</u> (b.1809) and <u>Thomas Lee</u> (1811) were born. Soon after the family moved to Lower Davis of Stoke Rivers where <u>Agnes</u> (1813), <u>Elizabeth</u>(1818), <u>John</u> (1820), <u>Ann</u> (1822) and <u>Susanna Lee</u>(1823) were born.
    The <u>1841 Census for Stoke Rivers</u> lists Mary Lee, age 60 widow, as head of the household indicating Thomas died prior to 1841.Mary Lee died late in 1862 or early 1863. She would have been about 80 at the time of her death. The <u>1851 Census for Stoke Rivers</u> lists Mary (widow: age 70) under the household of her son-in-law and daughter, Abraham and Agnes (Lee) Fry.

    A. <u>William Lee</u>:(b. 1809:Goodleigh) Around 1834 William married Susanna Davie, the daughter of Richard (b.1773:Goodleigh) and Susanna (b. 1779:Goodleigh) Davie, was born in Goodleigh about 1813.
    William and Susanna (Davie) Lee first made their home at Goodleigh where <u>Richard</u> (1836),<u>Susanna</u>(1837), <u>Thomas</u> (1839), <u>John</u> (1841), and <u>Mary Lee</u> (1844) were born. <u>Elizabeth Lee</u> (1846) was born at nearby Shirwell and <u>William</u> (1848) and <u>Henry</u> (1850) at Stoke Rivers.
    William Lee (1809) died prior to the taking of the 1861 census. Susanna (Davie) Lee is listed on the <u>1871 Census for Stoke Rivers</u> under the household of her son-in-law and daughter, John and Susanna (Lee) Fry. Susanna (Davie) Lee settled in Woodford Co.,Illinois (1873). She made the crossing with John and Susanna Fry. She is listed under their household on the <u>1880 US Census for Woodford Co., Illinois</u>. Her name does not appear on the 1900 census.

    1.<u>Susanna Lee</u> (1837), the daughter of William and Susanna (Davie) Lee, married John Fry.(See Fry Family in Appendix). They had at least five children. In America, their daughter, Emilie Lee Fry, married Frederick Newton Tallyn, the son of Anthony and Susanna (Lee) Tallyn. (Susanna Lee Tallyn was a sister to William Lee. See Susanna Lee in this section)
    2. <u>Thomas Lee</u>: (<u>1839</u>), the son of William and Susanna (Davie) Lee, settled in America around 1860. On March 16,1862 in Woodford Co., Illinois, Thomas married Grace Huxtable. She was the daughter of James and Frances(Ridge) Huxtable. Seven children were born to the marriage including <u>Hershell James Lee</u> who married Sarah Irene Tallyn, the daughter of Joseph and Sarah A. (Daniel) Tallyn.

****

B. Agnes Lee: Agnes, the third child born to Thomas and Mary Lee, was born around 1813 at Lower Davis of Stoke Rivers. Around 1838 she married Abraham Fry (See Fry Family in Appendix). At least 9 children were born to the marriage. Their daughter, Louisa Fry (1857), settled in America in 1873. Louisa married William W. Tallyn of Peoria County, Illinois. William was the son of Thomas R. and Elizabeth (Fry) Tallyn.

C. Susanna Lee: Susanna was the seventh and last child born to Thomas and Mary Lee. She was born at Lower Davis of Stoke Rivers in 1823. In Devon, England Susanna married (1848)............Anthony Tallyn. They sailed for America in 1848 settling first in Peoria Co. and then Woodford County, Illinois.

****

Some Additional Lee Family Data of Genealogical Interest:

The data below draws heavily from the records of Sheldena (Lee) Litle, of Harrisonville, Missouri. The author is indebted to Mrs. Litle for making her notes and records available for use in this document.

Some Children of William and Susanna (Davie) Lee:

1. Richard D. Lee: Richard was born about 1836 at Goodleigh. He was twice married. His first wife died in England. In America he married (2nd) Charolette (Lotty) S. Kent. She was born in N.J. around 1848. Three children were born to each marriage.

2. John (Jack) Lee: John married Mary Lake. Their children included: Herbert, Bessie, Sidney, Charles, Clara and Cora Lee.

3. Mary (Polly)Lee: (b. 1844: Goodleigh) She married a Mr. Holcomb.

4. Elizabeth (Lizzie) Lee: (b. 1846:Shirwell) She married a Mr. Hopkins. They made their home at Exeter (Devon),England. 4 Children Jack and Bill Hopkins settled in Denver, Colorado.

5. William Lee: (b. 1848:Stoke Rivers) He married (March 11,1869) Elizabeth Huxtable. She was the daughter of James and Frances (Ridge) Huxtable. (See Huxtable Family in Appendix) Their children included: Minnie, Denver and Freddie Lee.

6. Henry (Harry)Lee: (b. 1848: Stoke Rivers) He came to the US. around 1873. His wife was named Sally.

****

Of Historical Interest: The Lee Farm at Lower Davis of the Parish of Stoke Rivers originally consisted of 12 acres. Various tenants included: Thomas and Mary Lee, their son William Lee and wife, Susanna (Davie) Lee and John and Susanna (Lee) Fry. John increased the farm to 136 acres.

****

APPENDIX IV

THE FORNEY FAMILY [1]

******

Caroline Susanna Tallyn married (1892) Alfred E. Forney. Alfred was one of six sons born to Adolphus William and Mary A. (Diel) Forney. Adolphus was born in Pennsylvania as were his parents. Mary, his mother, was born in Maryland. Her parents were both born in Pennsylvania.

The 1880 US Census for Woodford (Clayton Twp.) County, Illinois lists the family as follows:

Forney, A.W.	age 49	B. Penn.	father: Penn.	mother: Penn
(w)Mary A.	38	Md.	"	"
(s)Harrison	19	Ill	Penn	Maryland
(s)Alfred	17	"	"	"
(s)Bertram	15	"	"	"
(s)Denver	12	"	"	"
(s)Elmer	5	"	"	"
(s) Charles	9	"	"	"

****

Adolphus was the youngest of seven children born to George and Elizabeth (Young) Forney of Hanover, Pennsylvania. George appears to be the son of Karle Forney (1810–1877), a third generation descendant of John Adam Forney.

The earliest of this family line in America was John Adam Forney. He came to the United States in 1731 from Switzerland. He settled on 600 acres which subsequently became the sight of Hanover, Pennsylvania.

Adolphus W. Forney settled in Woodford County, Illinois around 1854, In time he came to own several parcels of land in Sections 16 and 32 of the county. He gave the land for the Clayton Center School.

Around 1880 Adolphus built a three story barn on his property in Sec. 35 of Clayton Township of the County. His grandson, Emory O. Forney gives the following account of this structure:

> " ....My grandfather, A.W. Forney, was also a carpenter, and he built this three story barn, by himself. It was 28 ft. high to the plate, with stalls for horses on the ground floor and oat bins and storage for machinery on the second floor... with an approach from the East. The third floor was for hay and straw.
>
> It was a pretty red barn with white battons. A cupola on top let pigeons and birds in. They fouled the hay below and the cupola was later removed. In July of 1888 he sold the farm to Edwin M. Tallyn......."

---

1   Sources: Notes, Recollections and Memorabilia of Emory O. Forney, by Emory O. Forney, Minonk, Illinois, 1979, Unpublished mimeograph.

Historical Encyclopedia of Illinois:Peoria County,Vol. II, David McCulloch, Editor, 1902.

The Huxtable Family:[1]

The ancestral   home of the family is the North Devon village of
Huxtable. However, the 1841 and 1851 English   census for Devon
shows a number of families residing in Stoke Rivers and nearby Bratton
Fleming. The Huxtable family name has been long associated with
North Devon.

    James and Frances (Ridge) Huxtable were good friends of the Tallyns
of Devon, England and the Tallyns of Peoria and Woodford Counties,
Illinois. James was born in Devon (Dec. 31,1808) . He was one of
8 children. Frances was the youngest of 12 children. She was also
born in Devon (July 10,1826)..James and Frances were married in
September of 1848.   James was twice married. His first wife died in
England.

    The children of James and his first wife included: William F.
Huxtable (1839-1898), Richard A. (1840-1916), Grace Harriet (1842-
1891) Charity (1844-1846) and Charity Shoplin Huxtable (1847-   ).

    Children of James and Frances (Ridge) Huxtable included: Elizabeth
Frances (1849-1929), Sarah June (1850-   ), Phoebe Ann (1852-1935),
James Frederick (1854-1935), John Henry (1856-   ), Ida May (1858-),
Thomas Anthony (1860-1894), Martha Ellen (1862-1924), Fannie Anora
(1864-   ), Morris (1865-   ), and Flora Evadean Huxtable (1867-   ).

    James and Frances (Ridge) Huxtable lived out their lives in Wood-
ford County, Illinois. James died, September 10, 1894 at age 86.
Frances died August 18,1905 at age 79. Both were buried in Woodford
County..

****

Some Marriage Data of Genealogical Interest

Grace H. Huxtable	married	March	16,1862	Thomas Lee
James F. Huxtable	"	December	31,1885	Nora Peterson
Elizabeth F. Huxtable	"	March	11,1869	William Lee
Morris Huxtable	"	March	1,1887	Flora Younger
Martha Ellen Huxtable	"	_____		Frank E. Learned
Flora Evadeen Huxtable	"	_____		Ulrich B. Memmen
Phoebe Ann Huxtable	"	_____		Mr. Anderson

*****

Of Historical Interest

    William F. Huxtable and his brother, Richard A., were
in the Civil War.

---

[1]

    This section draws heavily from a two page mimeograph by May Bock
Brown. She was the daughter of Charity Shoplin (Huxtable) Bock. A
copy of this document was made available to the author, for use in this
work, by Sheldena (Lee) Litle of Harrisonville, Missouri.

APPENDIX VI

THE KINDIG FAMILY[1]

Interest in the Kindig line stems from the following marriages:

Charles S. Kindig and Lizzie Eva Tallyn (Feb.24,1886)
Theorodre H. Kindig and Alice Augusta Tallyn(Feb. 15,1893)
Bruce Henry Kindig and Alpha May Tallyn(Sept. 9, 1916)
Merton Dwight Kindig and Vira Kindig (June 24, 1927)
******

Charles Strwart, Theodore Henry and Bruce Henry Kindig:

The brothers Charles and Theodore Kindig were 1st cousins to John Martin Kindig....the father of Bruce Henry Kindig.

A. Henry Harrison Kindig: (1830-1914) Henry, the father of Charles and Theodore, was born in Augusta Co.,Virginia, January 5, 1830. On October 31, 1861, in Rockingham Co.,Virginia, Henry married Sarah Elizabeth (Betty) Spitzer. Betty was born June 25,1843/45 (?) Port Republic, Virginia. She was the daughter of _____ Spitzer and Martha Ann Fitch. The children of Henry and Betty included: Charles, Theodore, Mary E. (1864-1865), and Nellie Virginia Kindig (1874-   ).

B. Jacob J. Kindig: (1832-1920) Jacob and Henry Harrison were brothers. Joseph was born July 11, 1832, Augusta Co., Va. He was twice married. His first wife, Phoebe C. Zirkle (1838-1898) was born in Virginia. She died Juniata, Nebraska. Four and perhaps five children were born to the marriage. They included: John Martin (1858-1892); Charles Henry (1860-1932); Sophie (No Additional Data); Mary Ann (1863-1931) and Philip T. Kindig (1866-1939).
        John Martin Kindig: (1858-1892)   John was born in Clayton Twp. of Woodford County, Illinois, November 21,1858. He married (Nov. 21,1880) Ella Frances Lantz(Lance). She was born, May 8, 1861, McLean Co.,Illinois. She was the daughter of Absalom C. and Betty(Mack) Lantz. John died, Jan. 1, 1892 and Ella, Feb. 23, 1909. Both are buried Panther Creek Church of the Brethren Cemetery, Roanoke, Illinois. Their four children included: Omer Charles (1881-1936); Pearl (   );Phoebe (   ); and Bruce Henry Kindig (1891-1976). Bruce married(Sept. 9, 1916) Alpha May Tallyn (1893-1978).

Martin Kindig: 1797-1873/74 (?)   Martin, the father of Henry Harrison and Jacob J. Kindig, was born around 1797 Strasburg Twp. of Lancaster Co., Pa. He was one of 12 children born to Henry Kindig (1763-1825) and Maria Groff (1767-1842) of Lancaster Co.,Pennsylvania. Martin was twice married. He first married Susannah, the daughter of Peter and Esther (Herr)Pitmer. His second wife, the mother of Henry Harrison and Jacob J. Kindig, was Marie Stauffer (Mary Stover). Maria was born June 13,1789 (?). She was the daughter of Miachael and Barbary Stover. She died November 9,1859. Maria (and probably Martin who died Feb. 27, around 1874)) is buried Springdale (Mennonite) Cemetery near Waynesboro, Virginia.

Merton Dwight Kindig: (1906-1927) Merton, the son of Alice (Tallyn) and Theodore H. Kindig, married (June 4,1927) Vira Kindig. She is the daughter of LeRoy and Sally(Diffin)Kindig. She appears to be descended from a line unrelated to that of Charles, Theodore and Bruce Kindig.

---

[1]This sketch of the Kindig Line is based on data provided the author by Janet Smith (Mrs.Nelson J. Smith) of Metamora, Illinois.

APPENDIX VII

THE DANIEL AND CONIBEAR FAMILIES

Sarah (Daniel) Tallyn:

The following biographical sketch of the years of Sarah during her youth in England is based on the best information and research data available to the author. In England the family surname is spelled "Daniel" and not "Daniels" as is often found on various US records.

****

Sarah A. Daniel was born December 28, 1933 in Countisbury of North Devon, England. She was the daughter of George and Emma Daniel of Countisbury. She was christened in the Church of England, February 2, 1834. Her father was previously married to a woman named Amy. Two children Fanny Daniel (christened: Nov. 19,1826) and Joseph Daniel:(C)August 9, 1829) were born to this marriage.

Sarah was about 4 months old when her mother,Emma Daniel,died (i.e. April of 1834). Her father remarried (3rd). Her name was Eliza. The 1851 Census for Countisbury indicates Eliza age 43 was blind. This may account for Sarah being sent to nearby Bratton Fleming to be raised by her Grandpa and Grandma Daniel.

Around 1842 Sarah, age nine, was apprenticed to a dress maker known as Miss Christopher. She was a difficult task master who often worked her youthful charges well into the night making apparel for mourners. During her apprenticeship Sarah also attended school half days. Her long hours may have interfered with her schooling for her grandmother subsequently terminated her relationship with Miss Christopher.

In Bratton Fleming Sarah was well acquainted with the Conibear family. The Conibears lived nearby at Stoke Rivers. Sarah's cousin, Ann Daniel, married Thomas Conibear. Ann and her husband first made their home in Stoke Rivers and later at nearby Shirwell. It was probably after the completion of her studies that Sarah went to live and work for the Conibears at Shirwell. She worked as a dress maker..... making clothes for Ann and helped her in the care of her three children.

In 1851, at age 18 ,Sarah accompanied the Conibear Family to America. She helped with the care of the children during the crossing and later in Peoria County, Illinois, to help defer her transportation costs. It was at nearby Kickapoo of Peoria County that Sarah subsequently married (1855) Joseph Tallyn who had come to America some six months earlier in 1850.

There is but a slender store of data concerning Sarah's parents, grandparents, etc. The 1851 Countisbury Census lists Sarah's father, George and 3rd wife as follows:

George Daniel   age 56   Agricultural Laborer
  (w) Eliza   43   (blind) Born: London Limehouse
A niece, Mary A. Bales age 12 is living with George and Eliza.

Little is known of Sarah's mother, Emma, or of Amy, the mother of her step siblings Fanny and Joseph Daniel. Joseph is known to have made his home in Australia. Aunt Fanny Daniel is mentioned in letters of correspondence between descendants of Joseph and Sarah (Daniel) Tallyn. She lived to be quite elderly (mid 90's) and may have lived for a time in or near Ilfracombe of North Devon.

Descendants will be quick to note that the above sketch does not always correspond with bits and pieces of data concerning Sarah passed on by descendants to successive generations. Sarah was raised in Bratton Fleming but not born there...as frequently indicated. Some records have her arriving in America in 1854. Census records and her obituary notice indicate she arrived in May of 1851. This 1851 date is contrary to the frequently quoted 1854 date.

Daniel Familes of North Devon:

Loxhore, a small community about two miles from Bratton Fleming, appears to be the ancestral home of the Daniel families of this area. Church of England records indicate Alexander Daniel of Loxhore married (Sept. 20,1692) Mary Pugsley. It is of interest to note that Thomas Tallyn married (March 26,1787) Charity Pugsley of Loxhore. Thomas and Charity were the grandparents of Joseph Tallyn who married Sarah Daniel the subject of this sketch.

Several Daniel families are listed residing in Loxhore, Bratton Fleming and Countisbury on the 1851 and 1861 census years for these communities.. John Daniel and Joseph Daniel and George Daniel all list Loxhore as their place of birth. George, the father of Sarah Daniel, appears to be a brother to John and Joseph Daniel who make their home in Bratton Fleming. This assumption also finds support in the Church of England Christening Records for the three families.

The Family of Thomas and Ann Conibear of England and America:

Sarah's life, both in England and America, was inter-mixed with that of the Conibear Family. The children of each called each other cousin.

1851 Census: Shirwell of North Devon,England

Thomas Conibear	age 35	carpenter	Born: Stoke Rivers
(w) Ann	30	Keeping house	Bratton Fleming
(s) Edward	9	at home	Stoke Rivers
(s) William	6	" "	Bratton Fleming
(d) Elizabeth	4	" "	" "
Sarah Daniel(Dendel)	18	Servant:Dress Maker	Countisbury

Sarah and Ella B. Conibear were born to the family in Illinois.

****

Edward H. Conibear became a prominent merchant of Mineral (Bureau Co.), Illinois. Amelia , his wife, was born in England about 1847. Their children included: Chauncey, Hiriam, Frank and Rose Conibear.

William H. Conibear became a physician-surgeon. His first wife,Jane, was born around 1845 in Connecticut. Their children included: Amelia, Charles, John,Eric and Grant Conibear. Ruth B.,Lucy K.,Florence and Helen Coniber were children of William's second wife, Mary Bogardus. They made their home in Morton of Tazewell Co.,Illinois.

****

Christening Record: <u>Sarah Daniel</u>
Church of England

NAME / FATHER/MOTHER OR SPOUSE	SEX: M MALE/F FEMALE/H HUSBAND/W WIFE	TYPE	EVENT DATE	TOWN, PARISH
COUNTRY: ENGLAND	**COUNTY: DEVON**			**AS OF OCT 1976**
DANIEL, SALLY				
DANIEL, SALLY	PHILIP DANIEL/SALLY	F C	26JUN1797	EXETER, ALL HALLOWS ON
DANIELL, SAMUEL	JOSEPH DANIELL/	M C	09MAY1725	EXETER, SAINT MARY ARCH
DANIEL, SAMUEL	BENJAMIN DANIEL/MARY	M C	17FEB1733	EXETER, SAINT MARY MAJO
DANIEL, SAMUEL	BENJAMIN DANIEL/MARY	M C	15JAN1737	EXETER, SAINT MARY MAJO
DANIEL, SAMUEL	ANTHONY DANIEL/ELIZABETH	M C	24NOV1762	SHEBBEAR
DANIEL, SAMUEL	WM DANIEL/MARY	M C	18APR1782	SIDBURY
DANIELL, SAMUEL	WILLIAM DANIELL/CATHARINE	M C	01MAR1801	BRADFORD
DANIEL, SAMUEL	JOHN DANIEL/MARY	M C	01MAR1807	BIDEFORD
DANIEL, SAMUEL	JOHNES DANIEL/HONOR	M C	29JAN1812	BRADFORD
DANIEL, SAMUEL	WM DANIEL/ELIZ	M C	19JUN1814	BUCKERELL
DANIEL, SAMUEL	JOHN DANIEL/REBECCA	M C	04SEP1814	BULKWORTHY
DANIEL, SAMUEL	SALLY DALING	M M	26OCT1818	PANCRASWEEK
DANIEL, SAMUEL BADGERY	EDWARD DANIEL/HANNAH	M C	04JUN1815	HEAVITREE
DANNILS, SAMUEL PEARCE	/ELIZABETH DANNILS	M C	04MAY1783	HONITON ON OTTER
DANIELL, SARAH	AUGUSTINE DANIELL/	F C	19NOV1628	PARKHAM
DANIEL, SARAH	RICHARD DANIEL/MARGARET	F C	21FEB1663	AXMINSTER
DANELES, SARAH	/JANE DANELES	F C	12JUL1677	PARKHAM
DANIEL, SARAH	ABRAHAM DANIEL/	F C	22AUG1681	PARKHAM
DANIEL, SARAH	GILES DANIEL/	F C	25MAY1716	WEST PUTFORD
DANIEL, SARAH	JOHN DANIEL/	F C	02FEB1736	AXMINSTER
DANIELS, SARAH	NATHANIEL DANIELS/SARAH	F C	03OCT1744	OTTERY SAINT MARY
DANIEL, SARAH	WILLIAM DANIEL/	F C	24MAY1750	SIDBURY
DANIL, SARAH	JOHN GIBBS	W M	20JUL1773	LOXHORE
DANIELLS, SARAH	WM DANIELLS/	F C	22APR1775	SIDBURY
DANIEL, SARAH	ROBERT RENDAL	W M	1782	PINHOE
DANIELS, SARAH	JOSEPH DANIELS/RHODA CARSLAKE	F C	01JAN1787	SIDBURY
DANIELS, SARAH	JOHN DANIELS/ANN	F C	03JUN1798	HARPFORD
DANIELS, SARAH	JOSEPH DANIELS/ANNE	F C	11JUN1815	OTTERY SAINT MARY
DANIEL, SARAH	JAMES DANIEL/MARY	F C	21JAN1827	HONITON ON OTTER
DANIEL, SARAH	GEORGE DANIEL/EMMA	F C	02FEB1834	COUNTISBURY
DANIEL, SARAH ANNE	ABRAHAM DANIEL/JANE	F C	27JUN1832	PAIGNTON
DANIELL, SARAH BADGERY	EDWARD DANIELL/HANNAH	F C	17SEP1812	HEAVITREE
DANIEL, SARAH COOMBE	BENJM. DANIEL/MARY	F C	06MAR1764	EXETER, SAINT PANCRAS
DANIEL, SARAH ELIZA	GEORGE DANIEL/SARAH	F C	03NOV1830	ALPHINGTON
DANIEL, SARAH ELIZH	JAMES DANIEL/MARY	F C	01APR1825	PAIGNTON
DANIEL, SARAH MARIA	PHILIP DANIEL/MARIA	F C	29DEC1825	PAIGNTON
DANIEL, SELINE	JOHN DANIEL/JANE	F C	08MAY1825	BUCKERELL
DANYELL, SILVESTER	JOHN DANYELL/	M C	27AUG1599	PARKHAM
DANYELL, STEPHEN	JOHN DANYELL/	M C	27APR1606	GEORGEHAM
DANNELL, STEPHEN	THOMAS DANNELL/ELIZABETH	M C	01OCT1738	PARKHAM
DANNELL, STEPHEN	THOMAS DANNELL/ELIZABETH	M C	29FEB1744	PARKHAM
DANIEL, STEPHEN	HUGH DANIEL/ESTHER	M C	06OCT1747	STOKE DAMEREL
DANIEL, STEPHEN	THOMAS DANIEL/SUSANNAH	M C	28APR1771	ALMINGTON
DANIELS, SUSAN	JAMES DANIELS/MARY	F C	11JAN1820	BUCKERELL
DANIEL, SUSAN	JAMES DANIEL/ANN	F C	20MAR1825	THORNBURY
DANIEL, SUSAN BRIMACOMBE GEORGE DANIEL/MARY ELIZA		F C	17FEB1837	CLAWTON
DANIELL, SUSANA	SILVESTER DANIELL/	F C	30AUG1666	PARKHAM
DANELL, SUSANAH	JOHN DANELL/	F C	17DEC1672	DARTMOUTH, SAINT SAVIOR
DANIEL, SUSANNA	WILLIAM DANIEL/WARREN	F C	02APR1580	AXMINSTER
DANIELL, SUSANNA	JOHN DANIELL/	F C	22MAR1639	DARTMOUTH, SAINT SAVIOR
DANIEL, SUSANNA	JAMES DANIEL/SUSANNA	F C	24SEP1673	AXMINSTER
DANIEL, SUSANNA	JOSEPH DANIEL/	F C	23FEB1698	AXMINSTER
DANIEL, SUSANNA	NATHANIEL DANIEL/MARY	F C	04DEC1706	PARKHAM
DANIEL, SUSANNA	AGUSTIN DANIELL/MARTHA	F C	21MAY1717	YARNSCOMBE
DANIEL, SUSANNA	GILES DANIEL/JANE	F C	27DEC1722	WEST PUTFORD

B-BIRTH, C-CHRISTENING, M-MARRIAGE, N-CEN

THE HEIKEN FAMILY
By

Verna (Tallyn) Herbst [1]

A passport issued in 1880 indicates the Heiken family came to America from Roggensted of Ostfriesland, Germany. Anna Maria Heiken married Arthur H. Tallyn. Anna was one of four children born to Sjuit and Jabe Maria (Wertzen) Heiken[2] Sjuit Heiken as born, Feb. 4,1843 and Jabe Maria, Jan. 8,1838. Their children included: Maria , Heio, Johanna and John Heiken.

The turblent times of Bismark's Germany, including the German-Prussian War prompted....Sjuit to escape draft into military service by leading the family, under the cover of darkness, out of Germany and to the safety of America. The family survived the crossing which was marked by much sickness and death as severe storms caused high waves to crest the main deck and strong winds , repeatedly,pushed the ship backwards and off-course. The family arrived in America in the Spring of 1881. They settled in Woodford Co. (Clayton Twp.), Illinois.

Sjuit Heiken was a cobbler. He continued his craft in the town of Benson of Woodford County. The family were members of the German Luthern Church of Benson. Sjuit and Anna Maria (Wertzen) Heiken lived out their lives in Woodford County. Anna died, January 19, 1911. Sjuit died, May 16, 1916. Both are buried at the Benson Cemetery of Woodford Co.

Some Heiken Data of Interest

****

Heio Heiken: (1869-1943) Heio married Geske Broers (?)(1877-1918). Both Heio and Geske died at Benson , Illinois.

Johanna Heiken: (1872-1920) Johanna married Thomas Haig(1871-1911) of Woodford County . Both died in Benson.

John Heiken: (1873-1915) John served as the assessor of Woodford County. He died, December 23, 1915 in Benson, Ill.

Anna Maria Heiken: (1867-1951) Anna was born, April 22, 1867. She celebrated her 14th birthday aboard the ship which brought the family to America.

****

The 1900 US Census for Woodford County lists the Heiken family as follows:

Heiken, J.	b. Feb.1843	age 57	married 35 yrs	B. Germany
(w) Mary	b. Jun.1838	62	" " "	"
(s) John	b. Apr.1873	27	_____	"

****

---

1 Mrs. Herbst is the daughter of Arthur H. and Anna (Heiken) Tallyn. This article by Mrs. Herbst has been edited by the author for use in this text. See the family of Arthur and Anna (Heiken) Tallyn for additional data on Anna Marie (Heiken).

2 Jabe was first married to a Mr. Christopher, A son of the marriage, Henry Christopher (1861-1938),came with the Heiken family to America. Henry is buried at Benson,Illinois.

APPENDIX IX

McCUE AND JONES FAMILIES

****

Sarah Margaret(McCue) Tallyn was the great grand-daughter of the Irish immigrant, John McCue (1715-1775) and Eleanor Mathews. He came to America in 1737, settling ,first, in Maryland and later (1739) Virginia in what is now Nelson County.

John was the son of John and Sarah (McDowell)McCue and the grandson of John and Mary (Moffet) McCue of Scotland and Ireland. The latter John McCue was of the Covenanter or Presbyterian belief. He left his native Scotland to escape religious persecution. He settled in Ulster, Ireland.

Sarah's grandfather, Charles McCue, married Anna Maxwell. Charles was the fifth of eight children born on the original McCue land near Afton, Virginia. Charles was born in 1762. Sarah's father, Cyrus McCue was born (1810) on the McCue place near Afton. He married Frances Glenn. Cyrus suffered from deafness an infirmity shared by a number of his descendants in their later years.

Sarah Margaret (McCue) Tallyn, was the 12th of thirteen children born to Cyrus and Frances. All were born on the McCue farm near Afton. Sarah's brothers and sisters included: Ann Elizabeth (1851-1852); Charles (b1852); John W. (1853-1854); Cyrus Franklin (1855-1934); James A. (1856-1856); Moses Marshall (1857); Mary T. (1859); David K.(1861-1902);Bezaleel Maxwell (1863-1931); Samuel(1865); Martha Jane(1867); Sarah Margaret (1869-1963); and Permelia Fry McCue (1872- ?).

****

Etta Esther Jones (1895-1954)

Etta Esther Jones, the daughter of Francis Louis and Anne Rebecca (Bailey) Jones, was born near El Pasco, Illinois, September 9, 1895. Her father, Francis, was born on his father's homestead near El Paso, October 20, 1869. Her mother, Ann, was one of several children born to William and Elizabeth(North) Bailey. Ann was born near El Paso, July 17, 1873. Ann died, January 25,1937 and Francis, February 7, 1953.

Etta's grandfather, Cushing Jones (1824-1909),married (Apr.6,1848), Charlotte Brooks (1830-1916). Cushing was the son of Charles Jones(1786-1874) and Elizabeth Nichols (1782-1862). Elizabeth (Nichols) Jones, was a descendant of John and Priscilla (Mullins) Alden of The Mayflower fame.

Charles Jones was a great-great-great grandson of Robert Jones, the English immigrant ,who came to America prior to 1644. In Berkshire County, England he married Elizabeth Soane. Robert Jones died, November 17,1691.

Sources: (1) The McCue Genealogy, by Gertrude Porter McCue
                 Beatrice, Nebraska, 1941, mimeograph.

            (2) The Pictorial Genealogy of the Jones Family(Especially
                 the descendants of Cushing Jones)by Charles W. and
                 Herbert C. Jones, Easton, Kansas, 1969, mimeograph.

BIBLIOGRAPHY

I. <u>Formal References</u>:

Blackmoore, R.D. <u>Lorna Doone</u>, Dodd, Mead & Co., New York, 1943.

<u>Church of Latter Day Saints Genealogy Library</u>: Salt Lake City,Utah
and Santa Monica, California. (Census and Christening Records, Birth,
Marriage and Death Listings)

Jones, Chas. W. and Herbert C.,<u>The Pictorial Genealogy Of The Jones
Family</u>, Mimeograph, Easton, Kansas,1969.

<u>Los Angles County Library</u>: Genealogy Dept. Los Angeles, California.
(Woodford Co.,Illinois Biographical Books)

Loyn, Henry, <u>The Norman Conquest</u>, Pub. Hutchinson Co.,LTD, London,1965.

McCue, Gertrude Porter, <u>The McCue Genealogy</u>(Mimeograph) Beatrice,
Nebraska, 1941.

McCulloch, David(Editor),<u>Historical Encyclopedia of Illinois:Peoria.
County, Vol. II</u>, 1902

Moore, Roy L., <u>History of Woodford County Illinois</u>, Pub. Woodford Co.
Republican, Eureka, Ill.,1910.

Page, William (Editor),<u>A History Of The County Of Cornwall: Part 8
The Domesday Survey For Cornwall</u>, St. Catherine Press, London,1924.

Rice, James M., <u>History Of Peoria City And County Illinois: Vol. I</u> .

Rupp, Daniel, <u>German, Swiss, Dutch,French And Other Immigrants In
Pennsylvania (1727-1776)</u>, Genealogy Publishing Co.,Baltimore, Md.,
1956.

Smith, Janet, <u>Descendants of Henry (1763-1825) and Maria Groff (1776-
1842) Kindig</u>, (Mimeograph) Metamora, Illinois, 1979.

Stenton, F.M., <u>Anglo-Saxon England</u> (2nd edition) Oxford University
Press, London, 1947.

Sturgis, Ethel Adamson, <u>John Evans Adamson: Kill-Clifden, Conamara,
County Galway, Ireland</u>, (private printing) Portland, Oregon, 1957.

Vivian, J.L. (Col.),<u>The Visitations of Cornwall:Comprising The Heralds'
Visitations of 1530,1573 and 1620</u>, (Pub.) Wm Pollard and Co.,Exeter,
England, 1887.

<u>United States Federal Archives and Record Center</u>, Laguna Nieguel,Calif.
Source of 1900 US Federal Census for Woodford,Bureau and Tazewell Co's.,
Illinois, Military Records, Land (Federal) Purchase Records.

******

II. Informal References:

This work draws heavily from a wide range of less formal documents made available to the author by interested descendants and friends. In most instances they hold the status of unpublished mimeographs. They include, for example, compilations of historical and genealogical family data derived from bible records, obituary notices, church memorial programs, diaries, letters of correspondence, birth, christening, marriage and death records and headstone data. Some data stems from personal recollections, memorabilia and a tradition of oral family history and genealogy.....passed on (orally) by successive generations. Both Formal and Informal References constitute critical components of genealogy research.

The individuals listed below constitute major resources for the informal data used in this text.

Cochran, Annetta J. Manhattan Beach, Calif.	Bible of Joseph and Sarah (Daniel) Tallyn Notes & Records of William H. Tallyn
Davison, Vida G. Long Beach, Calif.	Notes and Records for family of Daniel and Mary Marcia (Tallyn) Davis
Finley, Elizabeth Rockford, Illinois	Biographer for the family of Roy C. and Harriet (Robbins) Forney
Forney, Emory O. Minonk, Illinois	Major Tallyn biographer with special reference on family of Anthony & Susanna (Lee) Tallyn
Herbst, Verna Washington, Ill.	Biographer for the family of Arthur and Anna (Keiken) Tallyn
Liebers, Mrs. Lawrence Lincoln, Nebraska	Notes and Records for the family of Ethel (Kindig) and Otto H. Liebers
Litle, Sheldena Harrisonville, Mo.	Notes and Records for the family of Sarah Irene (Tallyn) and Herschel James Lee
McPherson, Gracele Lincoln, Nebraska	Notes and Records for the family of Lizzie Eva (Tallyn) and Charles S. Kindig
Tallyn, DeWitt Benson, Illinois	Notes and Records for the family of Edwin M. and Sarah (McCue) Tallyn
Tallyn, Edwin W. Walnut Creek, Calif.	Biographer for family of William Henry and Mabel (Ellison) Tallyn
Tallyn, Milford G. St. Louis, Missouri	Notes and Records for the family of Frederick N. and Emilie (Fry) Tallyn
Tibbetts, Ella Edwards, Illinois	Major biographer for the family of Thomas R. and Elizabeth (Fry) Tallyn.
Thompson, Lelia Bakersfield, Calif.	Notes and Records for the family of Alice (Tallyn) and Theodore H. Kindig.

****